All American Stars

Eleanor shows her patriotism with the Americana Star! She gathered her scraps and pulled the wallhanging together with her very own Victory Garden fabric collection. She is looking forward to draping it over the banister to welcome guests to her ranch in Julian, CA.

Amie kept her quilting simple with continuous curve and quarter inch quilting in the blocks and cornerstones, rope quilting in the lattice, and a zig-zag variation in the border.

Eleanor Burns
Amie Potter
22" x 72"

Quilt Blocks on American Barns

Eleanor Burns

For Donna Sue Groves

Founder of the Quilt Barn Project

First Edition
April, 2010
Published by Quilt in a Day®, Inc.
1955 Diamond Street, San Marcos, CA 92078
©2010 by Eleanor A. Burns Family Trust

ISBN 1-891776-40-1

Art Director: Merritt Voigtlander
Production Artist: Marie Harper

Table of Contents

Introduction

I'm a city girl with my heart in the country! I was raised in the small German community of Zelienople, Pennsylvania. But every summer, I spent time with my cousin Carol Ann (Peffer) Selepec on the Wise farm in Harmony. There was nothing more fascinating than a farm. My fond memories include walking behind a baler and bringing in the hay. Our harvest celebration was a corn roast! We filled milk cans with water, lugged them to the hay wagon along with a huge black kettle and firewood, started up the old John Deere, and putted up the hill. I can still taste the tender corn, loaded with butter, fresh from the kettle.

What we remember from childhood, we remember forever! Old timers remember barn raising and quilting bees paired together as a social, exciting experience for people living in sparsely settled areas. In *Quilt Blocks on American Barns*, these two festive work-play events come alive again.

Join me as I wander through rural countrysides of America, one barn at a time. We're looking for bright-colored wooden quilt blocks mounted to the sides of barns and buildings along highways and country roads in small towns. The blocks, ranging from two to eight square feet, are painted in timeless quilt patterns.

This quilt barn project originated in Adams County, Ohio, with Donna Sue Groves of the Ohio Arts Council. I had the good fortune of meeting Donna Sue at Quilt Festival in Houston, Texas, in 2009.

Growing up in West Virginia, Donna Sue and her family would play a game of counting barn advertising signs, such as Chew Mail Pouch and Drink RC Cola, on long road trips. To pass the time, they would also discuss the different styles of barns as a history lesson.

In 1989, Donna Sue and her mother, Nina Maxine Groves, purchased a farm in Adams County. On the farm was a tobacco barn. Donna Sue promised her mother, a master quilter, that someday she would paint a quilt square on it for her.

In 2001, Donna Sue, along with help from The Nature Conservancy, decided to paint blocks on several barns to entice tourists to visit the county, stimulate business to local merchants, and create pride and teamwork within the community. It was a dynamic idea to combine farming and quilting heritage! In the summer of 2003, Maxine's quilt square, Snail's Trail, finally became a reality.

News of Donna Sue's project spread quickly to other communities. Her vision to create an imaginary clothesline of interconnecting barns decorated with quilt squares has grown into a National Quilt Barn Trail across the nation. Over 1,000 colorful quilt squares now adorn barns on the National Clothesline of Quilts that stretches across the US from Ohio and reaching to Kentucky, Tennessee, West Virginia, Iowa, North Carolina, Wisconsin, Indiana, and New York. More continue to join the Trail!

Bring the countryside alive! Share these barns and quilt blocks with your friends and family for generations to come.

Eleanor Burns

About the Quilts
Large and Small Barn Quilts

Eleanor Burns
Amie Potter
70" x 70"

Teresa Varnes
Amie Potter
40" x 40"

Farmers feature Barns with quilts as a way to get people into the countryside, share their love of the land, and honor someone in their own family. Combining a barn with a quilt square pattern honors quilting and farming, two important aspects of American life since colonial times.

In this book, both large and small Barn Quilts feature a large Monitor Barn with Windmill as the centerpiece. The large block is 26" x 18" finished size, and the smaller one is 18" x 12". It provides plenty of space for personal embellishment. I chose the Burns' family dogs, Peanut, Benjamin, and Tabatha for the larger quilt. The rooster is completely out of scale, but adds an amusing touch.

The barns in corners each reflect a different type of architecture. They include a Bank Barn featuring a brick foundation, a brick or stone Gothic Barn with curved roof, a Gambrel Roof Barn with Silo, and a weathered wood Dutch Barn. The Large Barn blocks are 12" finished size, and 6" finished size for the Small Barns. They can be placed in any position. Fussy cut animals cut from farm fabric add a realistic touch.

Between the four Barns are eight blocks. The large quilt has two 12" finished size blocks centered on each side. The small quilt has two 6" finished size blocks on each side plus a 3" block framed with Background. There are twelve to choose from in a variety of skill levels, and can be placed as you choose.

The space above or under the Monitor Barn and Windmill can be finished with blocks or a banner announcing American Barns. Letters can be hand or machine stitched with thread, or they can be fused in place and outlined with the blanket stitch. If you prefer, the large quilt features three 6" finished size blocks in place of the banner. Two can be duplicated for balance, or more may be selected from the thirteen available patterns.

The blocks are separated with Background Lattice, and framed with a narrow First Border. The Checkerboard Border is a tribute to Ralston Purina, leader in food for animals. The chickens and roosters strutting in the corners are fussy cut or raw edge appliqué, but can be substituted with blocks if preferred.

Lavender Hill Farm

Patricia Knoechel
Amie Potter
72" x 72"

Patty loves flowers, so she chose to plant fragrant lavender gardens around her barns. Her inspiration was gorgeous landscape fabric featuring beautiful women tending to their florals. She repeated three easy blocks and fussy cut the guardians of the gardens for center squares. Note the bank barn artfully turned into a charming cottage with lace curtains and window box. Patty's two favorite colors, purple and green, combine harmoniously like a soft medley. For a final touch, Debbie Gaarde stitched out the imaginary farm's logo on her professional embroidery machine.

The Funny Farm

Sue Peters
41" x 41"

Sue's preference is toward bright, cheery fabrics, so she was in "hog heaven" while sewing on this frivolous wall hanging. Cartoon-like oversized animals hang out on Sue's farm, giving it a comical nature. Chickens and roosters have something to crow about with their electrifying barns of orange, pink, and turquoise. Good natured cows chew on their cuds, contented to watch the world go by. You can't help but smile over Sue's whimsical quilt!

Country Roads

Diana Edgemon
72" x 72"

Diana loves the rich warm, natural earth tones of Kansas Troubles fabric line. The backgrounds blend perfectly with the logs in her summer cabin in Idaho. It was an easy decision to make her barn quilt for their log bed. She was happy to use up fabrics stashed about her home, needing to purchase only the backing.

Diana and her husband always wanted to travel the back roads of America following barn trails, a piece of Americana. Making this striking quilt was a way to live out her fantasies!

Additional Projects

Country Clothesline

Patricia Knoechel   *Page 118*
Amie Potter
12" x 13"

Winter is over! It's time to air out the quilts! Patty's easy to make wall hanging features a 6" Gambrel Roof Barn with 3" "quick quilts" cut from fabric.

Peaceful Pasture

Patricia Knoechel
Amie Potter
23" x 24"
Page 120

On Eleanor's Farm

Eleanor Burns   *Page 197*
Amie Potter
48" x 57"

Expressive roosters and hens strut about On Eleanor's Farm Quilt, exchanging local stories and juicy tidbits. A simple applique technique using paper backed fusible web gets the fowl chatting in minutes.

Serene barnyard animals gather round the 12" Gambrel Roof Barn, patiently waiting for their dinner. "Painted" on the barn is a stunning 3¾" Flying Geese Block. It's a charming gift for a country cousin.

Flying Kite Quilt

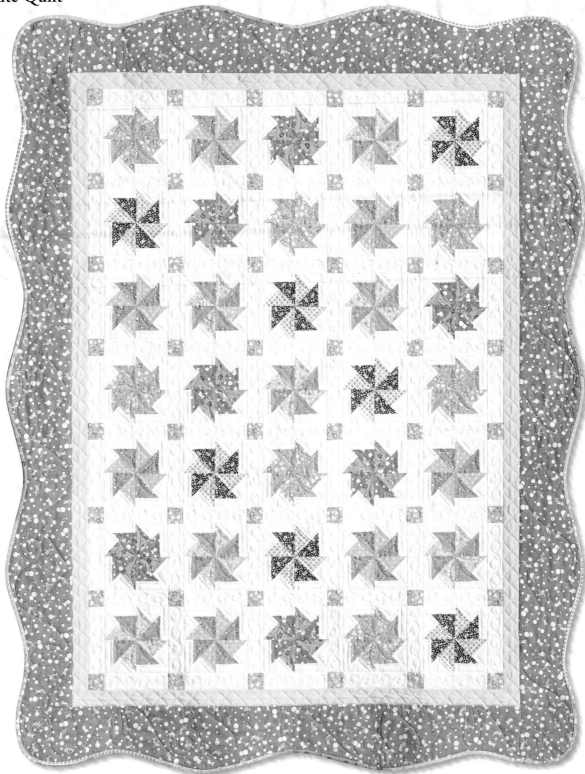

The quaint Flying Kite Quilt has the charm of a depression era
quilt, but sewn with all new techniques. Made of fabrics from
bygone times, the blocks are lined up in orderly fashion on a snowy
background with cheery cornerstones. The outside wave edge adds
an elegant touch!

Teresa Varnes
Amie Potter
52" x 68"
Page 138

Americana Star Wallhanging

Strike up the band with this patriotic wall hanging, perfect to use as a table runner or wall hanging on 4th of July! The fresh white stars boast of perky points, made simple using a special flying geese ruler. A colorful fabric repeated in the stars and border rings out "Stand up and salute! The flag is going by!"

Harvest Star Wallhanging

Teresa Varnes had a twinkle in her eye while designing this stellar wallhanging with 12" and 6" stars. Sunny yellow triangles combined with a sky blue folded border and binding complete the celestial wall hanging. Harvest Star is the most challenging block in *Quilt Blocks on American Barns*, but one of the most rewarding to successfully complete.

Eleanor Burns
Amie Potter
24" x 51"
Page 128

Teresa Varnes
Amie Potter
36" x 36"
Page 174

Fabric Selection

Most quilt blocks painted on barns are bright primary and secondary solid colors taken straight from a child's paint box. These colors are used so painted quilts can be spotted at a distance from the highway. If you prefer, richer country versions of primary colors can be used.

Select fabric in textures that read solid from a distance, mixing scales and values. Select suitable architectural fabrics that represent wood, brick, roofing, tile, and rock, plus ground, sky, and animals.

Purchase from this list of fabrics. However, the "hunt" for additional perfect fabric is fun, and can be ongoing. New fabrics can easily be introduced to this sampler barn quilt at any time.

Yardage and Cutting	Large Barn Quilt 70" x 70"	Small Barn Quilt 40" x 40"
Background	4 yds	1½ yds
Yardage is for Blocks, Lattice, Checkerboard, Chicken blocks, or Stars		
Sky	1 yd	¾ yd
Yardage is for Blocks.		
Ground	¼ yd	⅛ yd
Yardage is for Barns.		
Black	1¾ yds	⅝ yd
Yardage is for First Border, Chicken Blocks, and Binding		
Red	1¼ yds	½ yd
Yardage is for Checkerboard and Chicken blocks.		
Backing	4¾ yds	2½ yds
Batting	80" x 80"	48" x 48"
Paper Backed Fusible Web	1 yd	½ yd
Non-woven Fusible Interfacing	1 yd	½ yd

Fat Quarters

This is the minimum number of fat quarters needed to make your blocks.

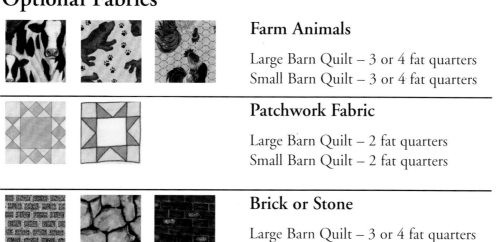

Red Include one texture for Barn.

Large Barn Quilt – 3 fat quarters
Small Barn Quilt – 2 fat quarters

Blue

Large Barn Quilt – 3 fat quarters
Small Barn Quilt – 2 fat quarters

Yellow Include one texture for Hay.

Large Barn Quilt – 3 fat quarters
Small Barn Quilt – 2 fat quarters

Green

Large Barn Quilt – 2 fat quarters
Small Barn Quilt – 2 fat quarters

Brown Include one texture for Wood siding.

Large Barn Quilt – 2 fat quarters
Small Barn Quilt – 2 fat quarters

Black Include one texture for Barn Doors.

Large Barn Quilt – 2 fat quarters
Small Barn Quilt – 2 fat quarters

Optional Fabrics

Farm Animals

Large Barn Quilt – 3 or 4 fat quarters
Small Barn Quilt – 3 or 4 fat quarters

Patchwork Fabric

Large Barn Quilt – 2 fat quarters
Small Barn Quilt – 2 fat quarters

Brick or Stone

Large Barn Quilt – 3 or 4 fat quarters
Small Barn Quilt – 3 or 4 fat quarters

Supplies

Basic Sewing Tools

Stiletto

Scissors

Rotary Cutter

¼ " Foot

Open Toe Foot

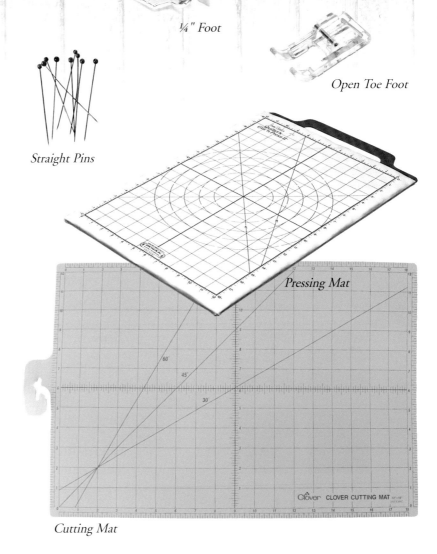
Pressing Mat

Cutting Mat

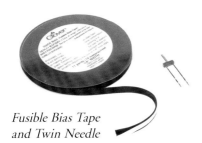
Fusible Bias Tape and Twin Needle

Straight Pins

Quilting Tools

Pins with Pin Covers

Kwik Klip

Darning Foot

Walking Foot

Rulers

InvisiGrip™

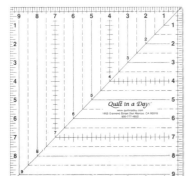

Cut a piece of InvisiGRIP™ ½" smaller than ruler. Place on bottom side of ruler. InvisiGRIP keeps the ruler from sliding when cutting.

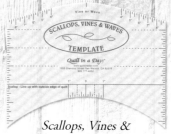

Scallops, Vines & Waves Template

Triangle in a Square Rulers

Mini Geese Ruler One

Mini Geese Ruler Two

9½" Square Up Ruler

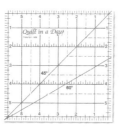

6" Square Up Ruler

6½" Triangle Square Up Ruler

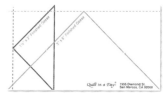

Small Geese Ruler

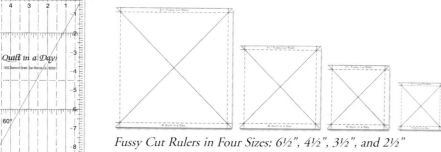

Fussy Cut Rulers in Four Sizes: 6½", 4½", 3½", and 2½"

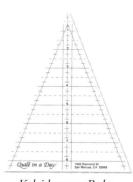

Kaleidoscope Ruler

6" x 24" Ruler

4" x 14" Ruler

6" x 12" Ruler

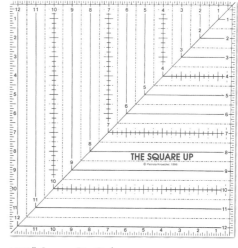

12½" Square Up Ruler

Cutting Your Quilt

Each block is shown with suggested color to use for each piece, plus the size to cut.

You can individually cut each block before you sew it, or you can assembly-line cut all blocks before you begin sewing. Once cutting is completed, each block takes approximately one hour or less.

Cutting Strips for Individual Blocks

1. Select designated fabric according to individual chart, and press.

2. Select ruler slightly longer than designated size. Best rulers to use for strips are the 4" x 14", 6" x 24", and 6" x 12" rulers. Straighten left edge.

3. Move ruler over until ruler lines are at newly cut edge. Carefully and accurately line up and cut strips at measurements given.

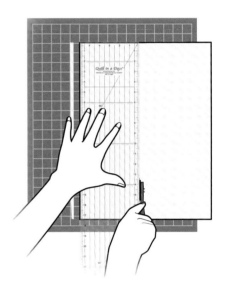

Cutting Squares and Rectangles

1. Select ruler slightly larger than designated size. Best rulers to use for cutting squares and rectangles are the 6" x 12", 6", 9½", and 12½" Square Up rulers. Place ruler on left corner of fabric, lining up ruler with grain of fabric.

2. Rotary cut pieces on right side of ruler, and across top, slightly larger than designated size.

3. Turn piece and cut to exact size.

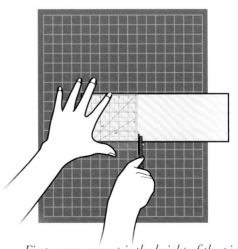

First measurement is the height of the piece, and second measurement is the width.

Cutting Directional Fabric

Barn blocks can be made with directional fabric for the Barn, Doors, and Sky.

Look closely at the block, and study each piece as you cut so the grain of the wood or sky are going in the right direction. In the Cutting Chart for directional pieces of fabric, **the first measurement is height, and the second measurement is width.**

Example of 12" Block

Sky

Before you sew, fold Sky in direction it is to be sewn, and check that Sky doesn't go sideways.

6½" x 3½"

Doors

The grain of wood in the Animal Doors goes up and down.

6½" x 3½"

3½" x 6½"

3½" x 6½"

Wood Grain

The Peak of the Roof is cut with wood grain going crosswise.

Example of 6" Block

3½" x 2"

3½" x 2"

2" x 3½"

2" x 3½"

Fussy Cutting Squares (Optional)

A Fussy Cut is a selected image, such as an animal, centered on a square.

There are four sizes of Fussy Cut Rulers™ available: 2½", 3½", 4½" and 6½". Perfect places for Fussy Cuts are centers or corners of your block, or Cornerstones.

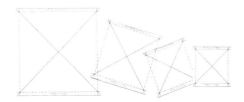

1. Select correct size ruler to match size of block. To keep ruler from slipping while cutting, cut InvisiGRIP™ ½" smaller than ruler and press on bottom side.

2. Find image on fabric that fits within size needed. Place fabric on small cutting mat.

3. Place ruler on image, with center of X on center of image. The dashed lines indicate the seam lines. **Shift ruler so image fits within seam lines.**

4. Cut around ruler with rotary cutter. Turn small mat as you cut.

5. To make your own template, cut appropriate size square from template plastic. Draw an X and ¼" seam lines. Place on image, draw around template, and cut out with rotary cutter and ruler.

6. Lay out Fussy Cuts in desired positions.

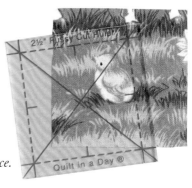

If necessary, place part of second image in seam allowance.

Fussy Cutting Tiny "Quilt"

1. Every barn block has instructions for a quilt block from 3" to 1½" in finished size. If you don't want to make a pieced block for the barn, fussy cut a block from "quilt" fabric.

2. Cut out square in designated size indicated on pattern and use it to replace pieced block.

Download printable quilt blocks on www.quiltinaday.com/eleanorandcompany/freepattern/

Raw Edge Applique

Fussy Cutting Animals

Try to find animals or barnyard figures appropriate to size of barn. Smaller animals such as chickens for 12" barns should be approximately 1½" tall. Larger animals such as cows should be approximately 4½" tall.

Animals for 6" barns should be approximately 1½" tall.

1. Rough cut around appropriate size animal.

2. Cut piece of paper backed fusible web slightly smaller than fabric. Make sure fusible does not hang over edge.

3. Fuse paper backed fusible web on wrong side of animal.

4. Cut out animal on outside lines. Peel paper away.

5. Fuse in place on barn block.

6. Stitch around outside edge of animal with straight stitch or zig-zag stitch and invisible thread.

Techniques

¼" Seam Allowance and ¼" Foot

Use a ¼" foot and ¼" seam allowance.

On most sewing machines, it's better to move your needle **one thread** to the right of center while using a ¼" foot rather than sewing in center needle position. A reduction of one thread width compensates for width lost in the fold of a seam.

For instance, when a computerized machine automatically sets itself at 3.5 for center, moving the needle one position to the right to 4.0 may give you the desired finished size of block.

Each block lists ideal sizes of pieces. If necessary, adjust needle position, change presser foot, or feed fabric under the presser foot to achieve that measurement.

¼" Foot

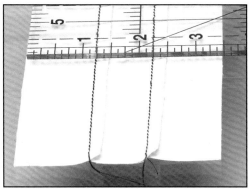

¼" Seam Allowance Test
Test your ¼" seam allowance by sewing three 1½" x 6" pieces together.
Size should measure 3½" from edge to edge.

Pressing

Individual instructions usually say which fabric should be on top, and which fabric seams should be pressed toward.

1. Place on pressing mat, with fabric on top that seam is to be pressed toward. Set seam by pressing stitches.

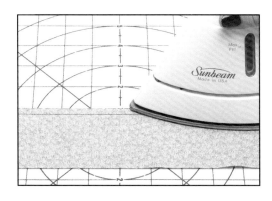

2. Open designated fabric and press against seam.

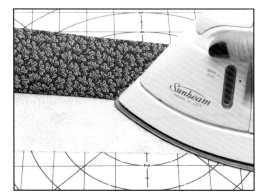

Finished Size

Finished size refers to size of block **after** it is sewn into the quilt. It does not include the ¼" seam allowance on all sides.

For instance, a 12" finished block is 12½" before it is sewn into the quilt, which includes the ¼" seams. A 6" finished block is 6½" before it is sewn into the quilt.

Once a block is sewn, uneven edges can be trimmed. Make sure the block is still ½" larger than finished size.

All blocks must be ½" larger than designated finished size.

Jumper Scrap

Before beginning to sew, remember to put fabric under presser foot, and needle down into fabric. Sometimes, beginning fabric jams into throat plate.

To avoid jams, start out sewing on a pair of 2½" squares cut from left-over fabric. Sew onto the patch right after the 2½" squares, and give a gentle tug if necessary to get the patch started. Collect 2½" jumpers, when you get enough, turn them into a Four Patch quilt. This way, you have something useful instead of a bunch of stitched over scraps that ultimately end in the trash.

Another solution to jamming is to use a single hole throat plate. Remember to change the plate when switching from straight stitching to zig-zag!

Squaring Up Triangle Pieced Squares

Triangle Pieced Squares are sewn oversized and need to be trimmed. This technique is called "squaring up". Use the Quilt in a Day 6½" Triangle Square Up Ruler to trim these blocks:

Hole in the Barn Door   **Cups and Saucers**

Corn and Beans   **Dora's Delight**

Hens and Chicks

One half of the ruler is used for trimming patches with ½" measurements from 1½" to 6½". These are marked with red dashed lines.

The second half is used for trimming patches with whole measurements from 1" to 6" marked in solid green lines.

Additional measurements are marked in ¼" or ⅛" increments **on the sides**. Red marks are ¼" lines, and shorter green lines are ⅛" lines.

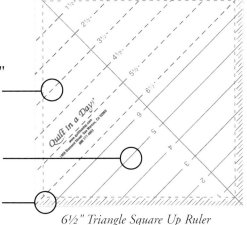

6½" Triangle Square Up Ruler

1. Place InvisiGrip™ on bottom side of ruler so ruler does not slide while trimming.

2. Stack closed triangles lighter side up.

3. Look for uneven edges. Freshly cut edges don't need to be trimmed.

4. Lay one test triangle on the cutting mat.

5. Each block indicates what size to square the patch to. **Lay the ruler's indicated square up line on stitching line.**

6. Line up top edge of ruler with triangle. Hold ruler firmly.

7. Trim right side of triangle, pushing rotary cutter toward the point to avoid damaging the ruler's corner.

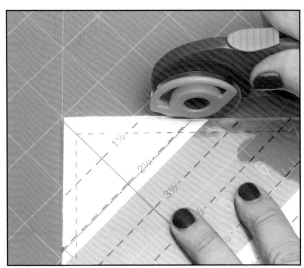

The example shows squaring the triangle to 2½".
The 2½" line on the ruler is on the stitching.

8. Turn patch. Trim tips with rotary cutter and ruler. From stitching, trim a 45° angle.

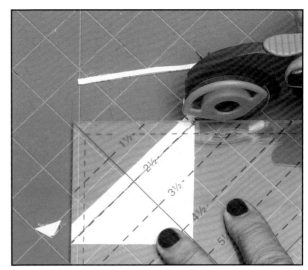

9. Tips can also be trimmed with scissors, using a 60° angle to assure that seam allowance does not show after triangle is pressed open.

   You can also trim tips after pieced square is pressed open.

10. Lay trimmed triangle on pressing mat, dark triangle side up. Lift corner and press toward seam with tip of iron, pushing seams behind dark side. Press carefully so pieces do not distort.

11. Measure with 6" Square Up ruler to see if it is desired size. If not correct size, adjust placement of 6½" Triangle Square Up. Place ruler line below stitching line if square is too large. If square is too small, move ruler line slightly above stitching line.

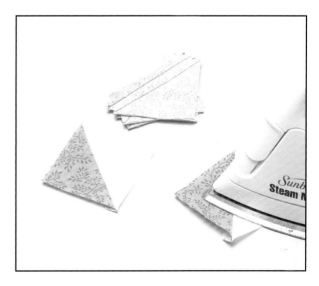

Flying Geese Techniques

These five blocks are made using the Flying Geese technique with Quilt in a Day Geese Rulers. Each block lists the finished size of Geese patch and the appropriate ruler. If you are new to this technique, the easiest block to begin with is Quatrefoil.

Mini Geese Ruler One

Mini Geese Ruler Two

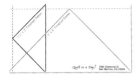
Small Geese Ruler

Quatrefoil – page 80
Use Mini Geese Ruler One.

Cups and Saucers – page 86
Use Mini Geese Ruler One.

Corn and Beans – page 92
Use Mini Geese Ruler One.

Flying Geese – page 106
Use Mini Geese Ruler One and Mini Geese Ruler Two.

Americana Star – page 122
Use Mini Geese Ruler Two and Small Geese Ruler.

 ## Making Flying Geese

1. Place larger Background square right side up.

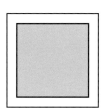

Each block designates what size to use. For instance, for 2" x 4" finished geese, the larger Background square is 7" square.

2. Place smaller Geese square right sides together and centered on Background square.

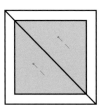

For 2" x 4" finished geese, the smaller Geese square is 5½" square.

3. Place 4" x 14" ruler on squares so ruler touches through four corners. Draw diagonal line across squares. Pin.

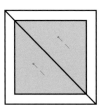

4. Sew ¼" from left side of drawn line. Use 15 stitches per inch or 2.0 on computerized machine.

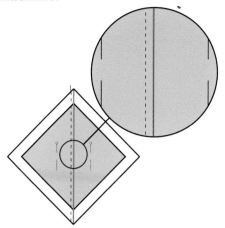

5. Turn. Sew ¼" from line on second side. Distance between two stitching lines is ½".

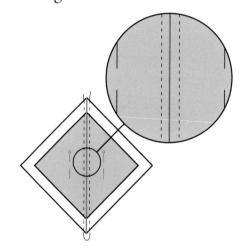

6. Cut on drawn line.

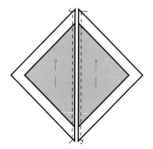

7. Place on pressing mat with large Background triangle on top. Press to set seam.

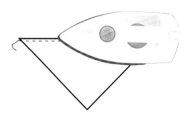

8. Open and press toward Background triangle, the largest triangle. Check that there are no tucks in seam.

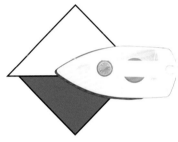

Press seam toward large triangle.

9. Place pieces right sides together so that opposite fabrics touch with Background to Geese. **Seams are parallel with each other.**

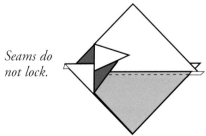

Seams do not lock.

10. Match up outside edges. **Notice that there is a gap between seams. The seams do not lock.**

11. Draw a vertical line across seams. Pin.

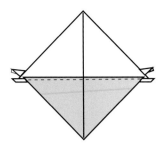

12. Sew ¼" from both sides of drawn line. Hold seams flat with stiletto so seams do not flip. Remove pins. Press to set seam.

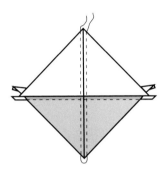

13. Cut on drawn line.

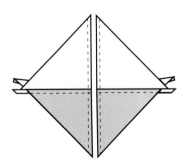

14. Fold in half and clip to stitching. This allows both seam allowances to be pressed away from Geese triangle.

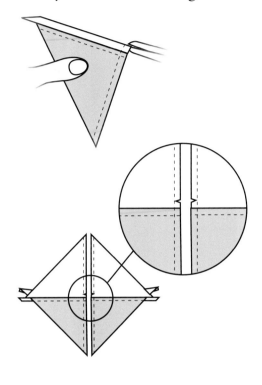

15. **From right side**, press into one Geese triangle. Turn and press into second Geese triangle.

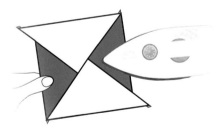

16. Turn over, and press on wrong side. At clipped seam, fabric is pressed in opposite directions toward Geese.

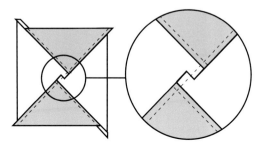

Squaring Up Geese Using Green Lines

1. Select designated size of Geese Ruler from Quilt in a Day. These directions are for trimming Geese using **green lines on ruler.**

2. Cut InvisiGRIP™ ½" smaller than Geese ruler and place on underside of ruler.

3. Place Geese patch on small cutting mat.

4. Line up ruler's **green lines** on 45° sewn lines. Line up dotted line with peak of triangle for ¼" seam allowance.

5. Cut block in half to separate into two patches.

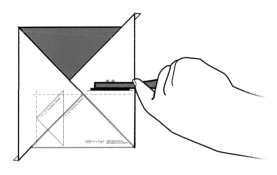

6. While turning mat, trim off excess fabric. Hold ruler securely on fabric so it does not shift while cutting.

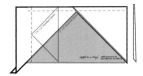

7. Check for ¼" seam allowance on top edge. Seams go into corners on bottom edge.

   Patches include seam allowance. This measurement is always ½" larger than finished measurement.

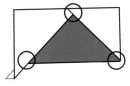

Squaring Up Geese Using Red Lines

1. Place patch on small cutting mat right side up. Place Geese Ruler in vertical position on patch. **Line up ruler's red solid lines on sewn lines for finished Geese.** Line up red dotted line with peak of Geese triangle for ¼" seam.

2. Hold ruler securely on fabric so it doesn't shift while cutting.

3. Cut block in half, and separate into two patches.

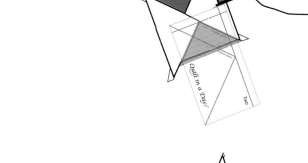

4. Trim off excess fabric on right.

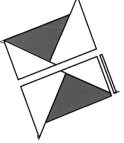

5. Turn patch. Do not turn mat. Trim off excess fabric on right and top.

6. Repeat with remaining half.

   Patches include seam allowance. This measurement is always ½" larger than finished measurement.

Monitor Barn
with Hole in the Barn Door Block

This striking Monitor Barn is on the property of Prairie Pedlar in Sac County, Iowa. Jack and Jane Hogue purchased the property in 1995, cleaned up trash and overgrown weeds, and removed tumbled down out buildings. They transplanted their garden business from their adjoining property, and now there are 75 beautiful theme gardens for visitors to enjoy. Once a year, you can view beautiful antique quilts displayed throughout the gardens. While you are at Prairie Pedlar, be sure to visit the Hogue's bow-truss barn painted with the Double Aster Block. www.prairiepedlar.com.

Hole in the Barn Door is known by at least twenty-seven names. Kansas City Star gave the block at least three, including the most recognized names of Monkey Wrench and Churn Dash, and unique name as The Crows Nest. The most unusual names are Dragon's Head by Woman's World and Bride's Knot, by Orange Judd Farmer, a periodical that offered patterns on the woman's page of American Agriculturalist.

Through the magic of computers and Photoshop, Quilt in a Day's Art Director Merritt Voigtlander "hung" the Hole in the Barn Door Block on Hogue's Monitor Barn.

Skill Level – Easy

Supplies

6½" Triangle
Square Up Ruler

*6½" Triangle Square
Up Ruler*

Make the 4½" Finished Block and 18" Finished Barn for Large Barn Quilt.
Make the 3" Finished Block and 12" Finished Barn for Small Barn Quilt.

	4½" Finished Block for 18" Finished Barn	3" Finished Block for 12" Finished Barn
Yellow		
Triangle Pieced Squares	(1) 2½" x 5"	(1) 2" x 4"
Center Strips	(1) 1¼" x 8½"	(1) 1" x 6½"
Blue		
Triangle Pieced Squares	(1) 2½" x 5"	(1) 2" x 4"
Center Strips	(1) 1¼" x 8½"	(1) 1" x 6½"
Background		
Center Square	(1) 2" square	(1) 1½" square

Making Triangle Pieced Squares

1. Place yellow and blue rectangles right sides together. Draw a center line.

4½" Block	3" Block
2½" x 5"	2" x 4"

2. Draw diagonal lines. Pin.

3. Sew ¼" from both sides of diagonal lines. Remove pins.

   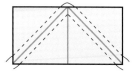

4. Cut on center line. Cut on diagonal lines.

   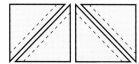

5. Square up Triangle Pieced Squares with 6½" Triangle Square Up Ruler.

4½" Block	3" Block
2" square	1½" square

Place 2" green solid line on 6½" Triangle Square Up Ruler **on stitching line**. Center ruler on patch. Trim two sides.

4½" Block

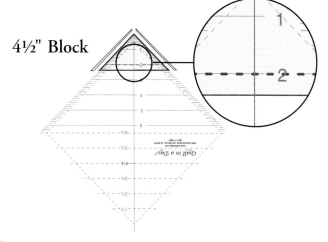

Place 1½" red dashed line on 6½" Triangle Square Up Ruler **on stitching line**. Center ruler on patch. Trim two sides.

3" Block

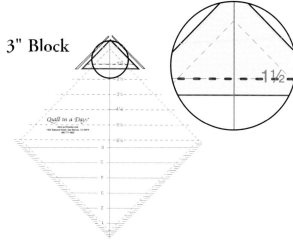

6. Set seam with blue on top, open, and press toward blue. Trim tips.

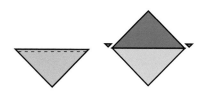

Making Center Strips

1. Sew yellow and blue strips together.

4½" Block	3" Block
1¼" x 8½"	1" x 6½"

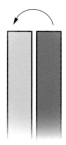

2. Set seam with blue on top, open, and press toward blue.

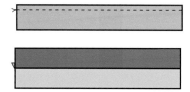

3. Measure width of strip set. Sliver trim or resew if necessary.

18" Block	12" Block
2" wide	1½" wide

4. Cut four sections into same width.

Sewing Block Together

1. Lay out block with Background Center Square.

4½" Block	3" Block
2" square	1½" square

2. Flip middle vertical row to left vertical row.

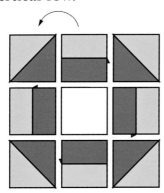

3. Assembly-line sew. Do not clip connecting threads.

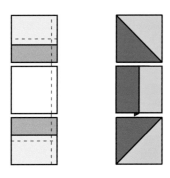

4. Open. Flip right vertical row to middle vertical row, and assembly-line sew. Do not clip connecting threads.

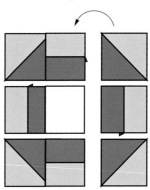

5. Turn. Sew remaining rows, pushing seams away from Center Square and Triangle Pieced Squares.

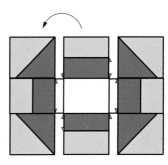

6. Press just sewn seams toward center.

7. Measure. Sliver trim or make adjustments if necessary.

4½" Block	3" Block
5" square	3½" square

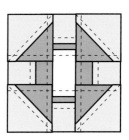

33

Monitor Barn with Windmill

Eleanor's family dogs, Peanut and Tabatha, keep the animals herded, while a stubborn rooster crows from the windmill. Notice the bracing on the double doors.

Patricia Knoechel substituted the windmill with a Lavender Garden complete with bird bath, feeder, and beautiful flowers. Notice the weathered directional wood on her barn and flowing directional blue/purple sky.

Michelle Countess outdid herself on her Monitor Barn. Clouds in clear blue sky billow over the quaint scene. The barn door, made of directional fabric, has narrow pieces of "bracing" to hold it together, plus hinges and a dimensional handle. Window frames are made of the same fabric. Open the door and you are greeted by a friendly cow and her young calf. Hay is hand stitched at their feet. Magnificent!

....

Supplies

¼" wide Black Fusible Bias Tape
4mm wide Twin Needle
Two spools Black Thread
Bobbin with Black Thread
20" Square Up Ruler
12½" Square Up Ruler

Optional:
18" Windmill
   1" Button or 1" Yo-Yo
12" Windmill
   ⅝" Button or ⅝" Yo-Yo

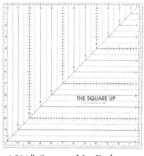

12½" Square Up Ruler

Monitor Barn	18" Finished Barn for Large Quilt	12" Finished Barn for Small Quilt
Directional Sky		
First measurement is height. Second measurement is width.		
Sides	(2) 9¼" x 5⅛"	(2) 6¼" x 3⅝"
Top	(2) 3⅛" x 6¼"	(2) 2¼" x 4½"
Windmill	(1) 16¾" x 9"	(1) 11½" x 6¾"
Wood Grain		
First measurement is height. Second measurement is width.		
Barn Door	(2) 7" x 2¾"	(2) 4¼" x 2"
Black		
Door	(1) ¾" x 7"	(1) ¾" x 4¼"
Side Roof	(2) 1" x 8"	(2) 1" x 6"
Top Roof	(2) 1" x 8"	(2) 1" x 6"
Directional Red		
First measurement is height. Second measurement is width.		
Tall Panels	(2) 15¾" x 2¾"	(2) 10¾" x 2"
Sides	(2) 9¼" x 5⅛"	(2) 6¼" x 3⅝"
Above Door	(1) 2½" x 5"	(1) 2" x 3½"
Top	(1) 3" x 5"	(1) 2½" x 3½"
Tan		
Ground	(1) 3¼" x 27"	(1) 2½" x 19"

Windmill	18" Finished Windmill	12" Finished Windmill
Lightweight Fusible Interfacing		
Stabilizer	(1) 8½" x 16"	(1) 6¼" x 11"
Windmill		
Blades	(1) 5½" x 6½"	(1) 4" x 6"
¼" Black Fusible Bias Tape	**2 yds**	**⅞ yd**
Legs	(3) 10½" pieces	(3) 6½" pieces
Door	Remaining Tape	(1) 3¼" piece
		(1) 2½" piece
		(1) 2" piece
Paper Backed Fusible Web		
Blades	(1) 5¼" x 6¼"	(1) 3¾" x 5¾"

Making Sides of Barn

1. Place two Sky Sides, wrong sides together, and two Red Sides, wrong sides together. Stack.

18" Barn	12" Barn
9¼" x 5⅛"	6¼" x 3⅝"

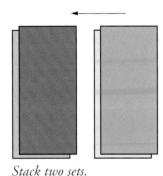

Stack two sets.

2. Make a mark from bottom up on left edge.

18" Barn	12" Barn
2¼" mark	1½" mark

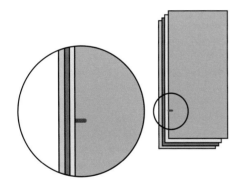

3. Cut from mark to bottom right corner. Discard triangles.

4. Remove Sky set.

5. Open Red Sides. Center Roofs on Red Sides.

18" Barn	12" Barn
1" x 8"	1" x 6"

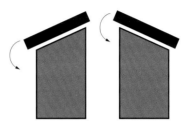

6. Flip right sides together, and assembly-line sew.

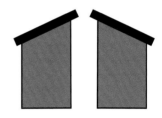

7. Set seam with Roof on top, open, and press toward Roof.

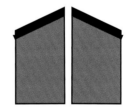

8. Trim Roof with Sides.

9. Lay out Sky with Sides.

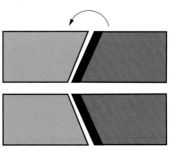

10. Flip right sides together.

11. Allow ¼" tip to hang out on both ends. Assembly-line sew.

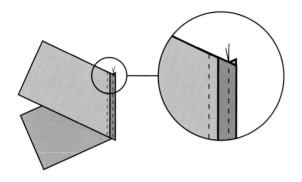

12. Set seam with Roof on top, open, and press toward Roof.

13. Sliver trim side with tips. Opposite side is trimmed in final squaring.

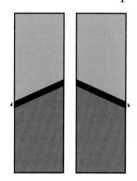

Making Barn Door

1. Place two Door pieces with narrow Door strip.

18" Barn	12" Barn
7" x 2¾"	4¼" x 2"
¾" x 7"	¾" x 4¼"

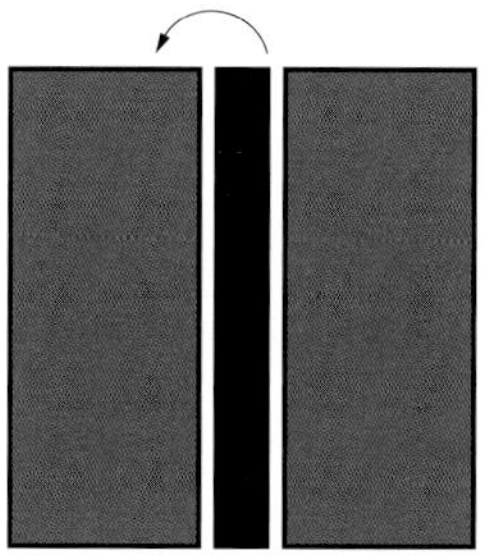

2. Sew right sides together.

3. Press seams away from narrow Door strip.

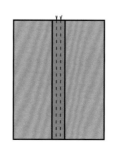

4. Measure. Sliver trim if necessary.

18" Barn	12" Barn
6¾" x 5"	4¼" x 3½"

Sewing Center Together

1. Lay out pieces with Door and block, and sew together with block on top.

18" Barn	12" Barn
3" x 5"	2½" x 3½"
2½" x 5"	2" x 3½"

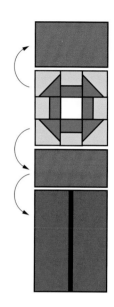

2. Press seams away from Door and block.

3. Sew Tall Panels to Center, matching at top.

18" Barn	12" Barn
15¾" x 2¾"	10¾" x 2"

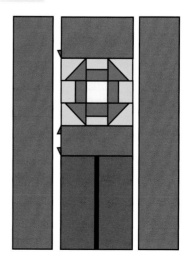

4. Set seams with Tall Panels on top, open, and press toward Tall Panels.

Adding Sky

1. Fold Center in half right sides together and crease. Open.

2. Mark down from top on both sides.

18" Barn	12" Barn
2¼" down	1½" down

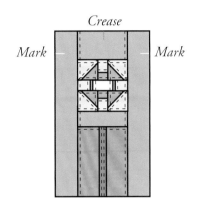

3. Cut from center crease to mark. Repeat on second side.

4. Discard two triangles.

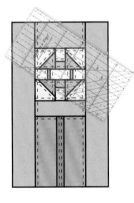 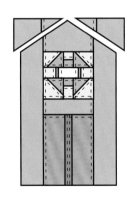

5. Center Roof on right peak. Flip right sides together and sew.

18" Barn	12" Barn
1" x 8"	1" x 6"

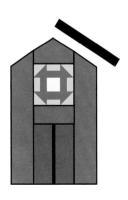

6. Set seam with Roof on top, open, and press toward Roof. Trim.

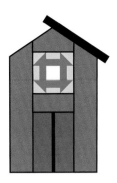

7. Repeat with Roof on left side. Trim.

8. Pair two Sky wrong sides together.

18" Barn	12" Barn
3⅛" x 6¼"	2¼" x 4¼"

9. Cut on one diagonal. Save the half with nicest clouds. Discard other half.

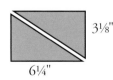

3⅛"

6¼"

Example of 18" Barn

10. Lay out pieces right side up.

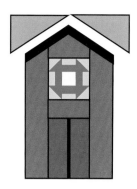

11. Flip right triangle right sides together, allowing ⅜" tip to hang out on right end, and sew.

12. Set seam with Sky on top, open, and press toward Sky. Trim tip.

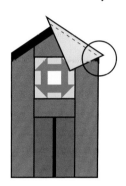 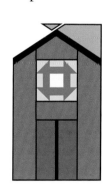

13. Flip left triangle right sides together, allowing ¼" tip to hang out on left end, and sew.

14. Set seam with Sky on top, open, and press toward Sky.

15. Square Sky, leaving ¼" seam allowance.

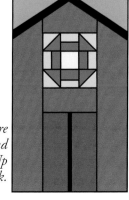

Square Sky using 9½" Square Up Ruler for 18" Block, and 6½" Triangle Square Up Ruler for 12" Block.

Finishing Barn

1. Lay out center of Barn with two Sides.

2. Match Sides to center of Barn on top, and sew from top down. Press seams toward Sides.

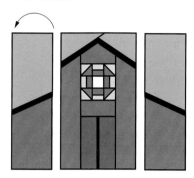

3. Straighten bottom edge only.

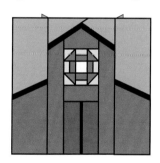

4. Fuse bracing on Door with fusible bias tape. Peel paper from tape.

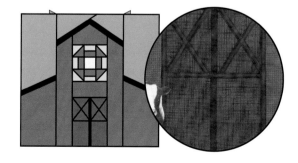

- It helps if you cut ends of bias tape on diagonal. Fuse X on top half of each side.

- Fuse piece across center.

- Fuse pieces around outside edge of Door.

Making Legs for Windmill

1. Fuse stabilizer to wrong side of Sky.

2. Place Placement Sheet on pressing mat.

18" Barn	12" Barn
8½" x 16"	6¼" x 11"

3. Place Sky fabric on Placement sheet, right side up with left side and bottom edge lined up with placement sheet.

4. Peel paper from bias tape strips, and arrange on Leg lines. Cut to length. Remove Placement Sheet. Press in place.

Sewing Bias Tape with Twin Needle

The easiest way to secure bias tape is to sew down both edges of tape at the same time with a twin needle. Bias tape can also be edge stitched one side at a time with a single needle.

1. Place ⅛" wide twin needle and two spools of thread on sewing machine.

2. Run thread from two spools at the same time to needles. Thread each needle separately.

3. Place bobbin with matching thread in bobbin case.

4. Sew down center of bias tape on Windmill legs and Door of Barn. Press.

5. Fuse Cross Braces of bias tape for 6" Windmill block and sew.

Tracing Blades

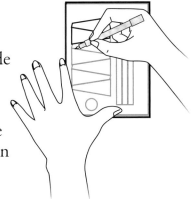

1. Place Pattern Sheet right side up.

2. Place paper backed fusible web on Pattern Sheet, paper side up.

3. Trace strips for blades and Cross Braces. Round Center is optional. You can use a button in place of a circle of fabric.

Fusing Blades

1. Place Windmill fabric on pressing mat, wrong side up.

2. Center traced patterns on fabric, paper side up.

3. Fuse in place for two seconds without steam.

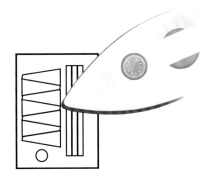

4. Cut out pieces on traced lines **with ruler and rotary cutter.**

5. Peel paper from pieces and arrange on Sky, following lines on Placement Sheet. Remove Placement Sheet.

6. Fuse in place for eight seconds without steam.

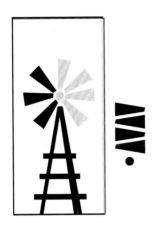

Sewing Edges with Satin Stitch

1. Place a single needle and one spool of thread on your machine. **Put matching thread in bobbin.**

2. Select a zigzag stitch. Set stitch width at approximately 3.0 and stitch length at 0.3 for a narrow, closely spaced stitch.

3. Start in the middle of one side. Place needle in fabric on edge.

4. Sew to corner, with stitches going back and forth, covering raw edge.

5. Stop at corner, with needle down on outside edge of corner.

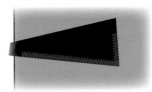

6. Pivot with needle in fabric. Start stitching again.

7. New stitches cover previous stitches on corner. Sew to end, and lock stitches.

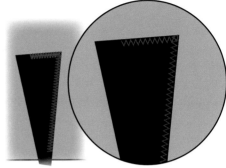

8. Square up Windmill.

18" Barn	12" Barn
16½" x 8½"	11¼"x 6½"

Sewing Windmill to Barn

1. Pin and sew Windmill to Barn. Press seam toward Windmill. Trim excess if necessary.

2. Sew Ground to bottom edge. Press seam toward Ground. Trim excess if necessary.

18" Barn	12" Barn
3¼ " x 27"	2½" x 19"

3. Add selected images to block with raw edge applique technique, page 21.

Dutch Barn
with End of the Day Block

Dutch barns represent the oldest and rarest types of barns. They were the first great barns built in America by Dutch settlers in the Hudson River Valley, New York, from late 1600's through 1800's. There are relatively few—probably less than 600—of these barns still intact. Common features of these barns include a gabled roof, paired wagon doors on the gable ends with a pentice roof over them, and smaller animal doors at the corners. Dutch barns often lacked windows and had no openings other than the doors and martin holes on gable ends for ventilation. Left unpainted, some Dutch Barns are still standing today.

The End of the Day block originally appeared in the Farm Journal, a periodical established in March, 1877. Farm Journal has absorbed at least three other pattern sources: Country Gentleman, The Farmers Wife and Household Journal. The End of the Day block was placed on this barn with Photoshop, a computer program.

photo – Kim Balfour

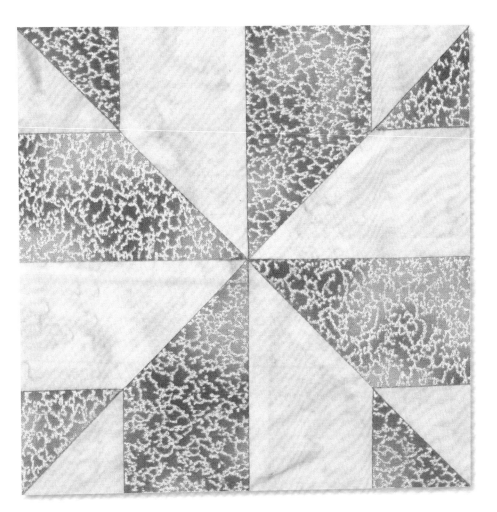

Skill Level – Easy

Supplies
   6" Square Up Ruler
   6" x 12" Ruler

6" Square Up Ruler

6" x 12" Ruler

	6" Finished Block for Quilt	3" Finished Block for 12" Finished Barn	1½" Finished Block for 6" Finished Barn
Blue			
Dark	(1) 2¼" x 34"	(1) 1½" x 21"	(1) 1⅛" x 16"
Yellow			
Light	(1) 2¼" x 34"	(1) 1½" x 21"	(1) 1⅛" x 16"
Optional Fussy Cut Square			
Fussy Cut "Quilt"		(1) 3½" square	(1) 2" square

Making End of the Day Block

Sewing Strips

One set of strips makes two mirror image blocks.

1. Lay out strips with dark on right.

6" Block	3" Block	1½" Block
2¼" x 34"	1½" x 21"	1⅛" x 16"

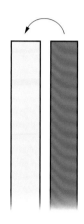

2. Flip dark strip right sides together to light, and sew.

3. Set seam with dark on top, open, and press toward dark.

4. Cut strip set in half into two equal sets.

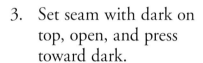

5. Place strip sets right sides together with dark across top, and lock seams.

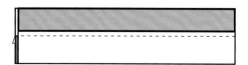

6. Square left end. Cut into four squares.

6" Block	3" Block	1½" Block
4" squares	2½" squares	1¾" squares

7. Draw a pencil line diagonally from corner to corner across each square. **Every square must be marked the same.**

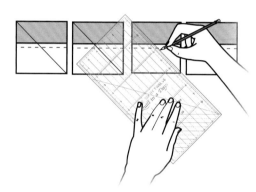

8. Lock top seam to underneath seam. See circle.

9. Assembly-line sew ¼" from pencil line on left side.

10. Turn patches around and assembly-line sew ¼" from pencil line on remaining side.

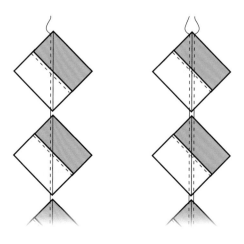

Laying Out Squares

1. Lay out square with dark across top.

2. Cut on pencil line, cutting square into two triangles.

3. Carefully stack in **two separate piles**. Always place small triangles to left.

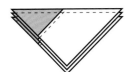 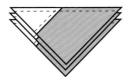

4. Place on pressing mat with seam across top.

5. Set seam, open, and press toward seam.

 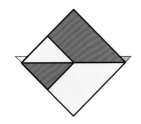

6. Place smallest triangles in upper right corner.

7. Square patch with 6" Square Up Ruler.

6" Block	3" Block	1½" Block
3½" square	2" square	1¼" square

Example of 2" Square

 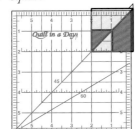

Place smallest triangles in upper right corner. *Place diagonal line on seam. Trim tip.*

Turn patch. Do not turn ruler. Place squaring lines on outside edges. Trim right and top edges.

Sewing Block Together

1. From one stack, lay out a block. Turn points of smallest triangles toward outside edges.

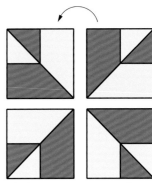

Blocks are mirror image from each other. Sew both blocks and choose the one that looks the best for the Barn block.

2. Flip vertical row on right to vertical row on left.

3. Lock seams and assembly-line sew. Do not clip connecting thread.

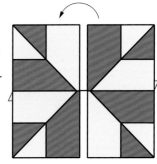

4. Open, and turn. Flip vertical row on right to vertical row on left.

5. At center seam, push top seam up and underneath seam down.

6. Assembly-line sew.

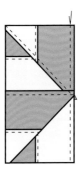

7. At center seam, cut first stitch with scissors. See red stitches in circle.

8. Remove **three straight stitches** in seam on both sides with stiletto or seam ripper.

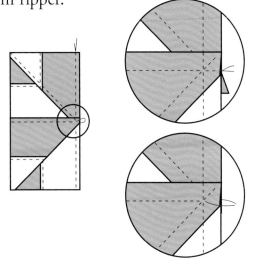

9. Open center seams and "swirl" to form a tiny pinwheel.

10. Press seams clockwise around center.

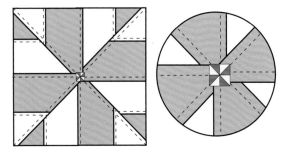

11. Square block.

6" Block	3" Block	1½" Block
6½" square	3½" square	2" square

12. Sew second block. Select the nicest one.

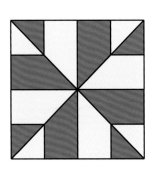 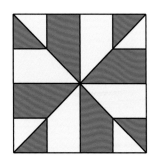

Anne Tracy selected fabrics in yellow and blue for a midday block. In place of using directional wood fabric, Anne stitched in horizontal boards. The wagon door looks massive with it's impressive stitching… and the cow is a perfect scale to match the animal door!

Julie Greenspan created an entertaining Dutch Barn in polka dot fabric, and selected cartoon animals to complete the barnyard scene. Diagonal lines quilted on the barn emphasizes the steep pitch in the roof. Cute!

Anne Tracy
31" x 36"

Anne chose to leave off the checkerboard border so her delightful wallhanging fits in a small space. Her precisely stitched 6" blocks are well balanced around the 12" Monitor Barn and Windmill. She quilted a continuous loop on the wide Lattice, a sky meander on the central block, and free motion quilting on individual blocks. The bright red binding is a perfect ending for a perfect quilt.

Dutch Barn

Chris Levine planted a horse peering out the top half of the giant Dutch door. The top door actually opens and closes. A leaning pitchfork appears to be propping the door open.

A beautiful blue sky outlines the steep roof line on Eleanor Burns' Dutch barn. Notice the directional fabric on both the barn and wagon door, replicating the wood on old Dutch barns.

Inspired by fabric that looks like stained glass, Patty Knoechel turned her Dutch barn into a moonlit Chapel. She shortened the wagon door so the chapel door wasn't quite so tall, and appliquéd stained glass windows on the stone chapel. Trees are appliquéd in two layers, with fabric in the closest layer right side up, and the farthest layer wrong side up to give the illusion of distance. Quilting in the fluffy snow appears as gust of wind.

Moonlit Chapel

Patricia Knoechel
Amie Potter
20" x 22"

Skill Level – Easy

Supplies
12½" Square Up Ruler
6½" Triangle Square Up Ruler

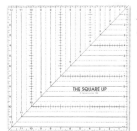

12½" Square Up Ruler

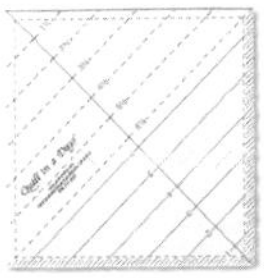

6½" Triangle Square Up Ruler

	12" Finished Barn	6" Finished Barn
Directional Barn First measurement is height. Second measurement is width.		
Peak of Roof	(1) 3½" x 6½"	(1) 2" x 3½"
Roof	(2) 3½" squares	(2) 2" squares
Sides of Quilt	(2) 3½" x 2"	(2) 2¼" x 1¼"
Top of Animal Doors	(2) 2⅞" x 4½"	(2) 1½" x 2½"
Sides of Animal Doors	(2) 3" squares	(2) 1¾" squares
Pentice	(1) 1" x 4½"	(1) ¾" x 2½"
Directional Sky First measurement is height. Second measurement is width.		
Peak of Roof	(6) 3½" squares	(6) 2" squares
Green		
Ground	(1) 2½" x 12¾"	(1) 1¾" x 6¾"
Wood Grain First measurement is height. Second measurement is width.		
Animal Doors	(2) 3" x 2"	(2) 1¾" x 1¼"
One Piece Wagon Door	(1) 5" x 4½"	(1) 2½" square
Or Dutch Doors		
Left Wagon Door	(1) 5" x 2½"	(1) 2½" x 1½"
Bottom Half of Right Dutch Door	(1) 2¾" x 2½"	(1) 1½" square
Open Dutch Door	(2) 2½" squares	(2) 1½" squares
Yellow		
Top Half of Right Dutch Door	(1) 2½" square	(1) 1½" square

Fussy Cut Animals and Paper Backed Fusible Web

Making Dutch Barn

Sewing Parts of Roof

1. Turn four Sky squares wrong side up. Draw diagonal lines.

12" Block	6" Block
3½" squares	2" squares

   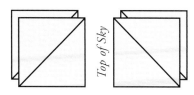

2. Place one Sky square right sides together to Peak of Roof. Sew on drawn line.

12" Block	6" Block
3½" x 6½"	2" x 3½"

   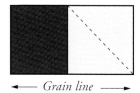

   ← Grain line →

3. Trim ¼" from line.

4. Press seam toward Sky.

5. Place Sky square on Roof. Sew on line.

6. Trim ¼" from line.

7. Press seam toward Sky.

8. Place grain line on Roof squares crosswise.

   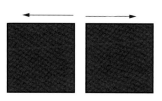

9. Place same size Sky squares right sides together to Roof squares. **Sew on drawn lines.**

   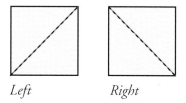

   Left   *Right*

10. Trim ¼" from line.

    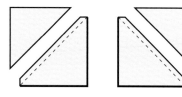

11. Set seam with Roof on top, open, and press toward Roof.

    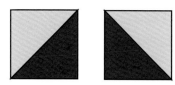

12. Check measurements.

12" Block	6" Block
3½" square	2" square

13. Sew Quilt to Sides wrong side up so seams don't twist.

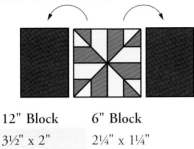

12" Block   **6" Block**
3½" x 2"   2¼" x 1¼"

14. Press seams toward Sides, and trim even.

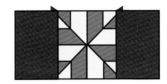

Sewing Roof Together

1. Lay out Roof with Sky squares and Quilt unit.

12" Block   **6" Block**
3½" squares   2" squares

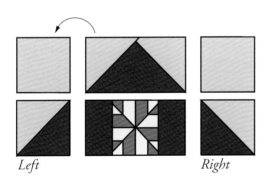

Left   *Right*

2. Flip middle vertical row right sides together to left vertical row, and assembly-line sew. Do not clip apart.

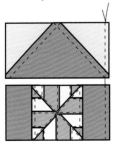 

3. Flip right vertical row to middle vertical row, and assembly-line sew. Do not clip apart.

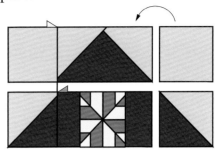

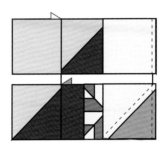

4. From wrong side, press seams toward Sky on top row, and toward Quilt on second row.

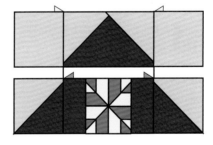

5. Sew rows together, locking seams.

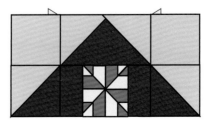

6. Press seams toward top row.

Sewing Animal Doors

1. Lay out Animal Doors with Sides and sew together.

12" Block	6" Block
3" x 2"	1¾" x 1¼"
3" squares	1¾" squares

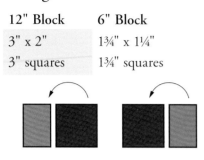

2. Press seams toward Doors.

3. Sew Top to Doors and press toward Top.

12" Block	6" Block
2⅞" x 4½"	1½" x 2½"

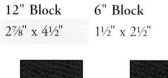

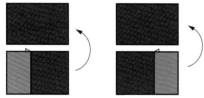

Sewing One Piece Wagon Door to Animal Doors

1. Lay out Wagon Door with Pentice.

Door	5" x 4½"	2½" square
Pentice	1" x 4½"	¾" x 2½"

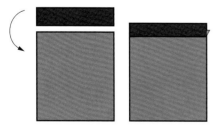

2. Sew together, and press seam toward Pentice.

3. Sew Wagon Door to Animal Doors.

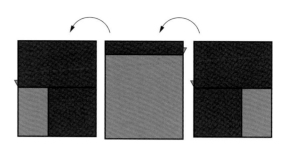

4. Press seams away from Wagon Door.

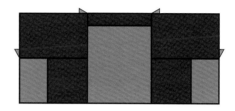

5. Trim bottom edge if needed.

Sewing Optional Dutch Door

1. Lay out Dutch Door. Optional: Fuse head of animal in open door.

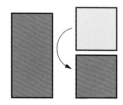

2. Sew top half of right Dutch Door to bottom half of right Dutch Door.

Top Half	2½" square	1½" square
Bottom Half	2¾" x 2½"	1½" square

3. Press seam toward Bottom Door.

4. Sew to Left Wagon Door.

12" Block	6" Block
5" x 2½"	2½" x 1½"

5. Press to Left Side.

6. Sew Pentice to top of Door.

12" Block	6" Block
1" x 4½"	¾" x 2½"

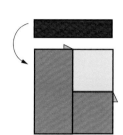

7. Press toward Pentice.

8. Place two Open Dutch Door squares right sides together. Sew three sides.

12" Block	6" Block
2½" squares	1½" squares

9. Turn right out. Push out corners.

10. Pin Open Dutch Door below Pentice, lining up raw edges on right.

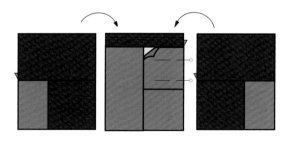

11. Sew Animal Doors to Open Dutch Door.

12. Press seams away from Wagon Door.

13. Press Open Door to the right.

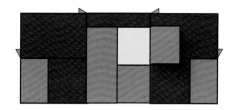

14. Trim bottom edge if needed.

Sewing Barn Together

1. Sew two Barn units together with Ground unit. Press seams down.

2½" x 12¾"	1¾" x 6¾"

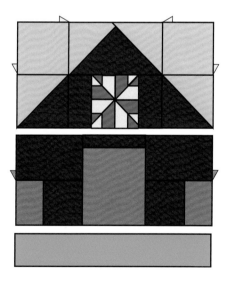

2. Fuse fussy cut animals in place and sew around outside edges.

3. Square up block.

12" Block	6" Block
12½" square	6½" square

Broken Wheel Block

Broken Wheel Block proudly hangs on a drive-through barn at Davidson Farm in Rogersville, TN. The block, in bright oranges and yellow complemented by black, reflects the importance of the rich-hued fall harvest season to their family. School children can visit the farm and tour pumpkin fields and a "haunted" maze, plus attend pre-Halloween happenings in "Pumpkin Valley." The fourth generation family farm shares their agriculture heritage with the public, including a large variety of produce and seasonal items.

It was the final barn in the first segment of the Appalachian Quilt Trail. You can take a scenic driving tour along the Trail and explore the beauty and tranquility of East Tennessee's historic byways, plus stop and visit The Davidson Farm.

The Broken Wheel Block was originally published by the Dakota Farmer in 1929, a periodical established in 1881 in Aberdeen, SD in the late 1920's. It had a unique quilt column with readers sending in designs. In the same year, it was renamed Corn Design by Dakota Farmer. Woman's World named it Old Crow, while Carrie Hall, in *Romance of the Patchwork Quilt in America*, called it Crow's Foot.

www.thedavidsonfarm.com
www.vacationaqt.com

Skill Level – Easy

....

Supplies

12" Block
4½" Fussy Cut Ruler

4½" Fussy Cut Ruler

6" Block
2½" Fussy Cut Ruler

2½" Fussy Cut Ruler

	12" Finished Block	6" Finished Block
Background		
Center	(1) 4½" square or (1) 4½" Fussy Cut	(1) 2½" square or (1) 2½" Fussy Cut
Corners	(2) 3½" squares	(2) 2½" squares
Yellow		
Corners	(1) 3½" x 22" cut into (6) 3½" squares	(1) 2½" x 16" cut into (6) 2½" squares
Light Green		
Stripe	(1) 2½" x 19"	(1) 1½" x 11"
Dark Green		
Stripe	(1) 2½" x 19"	(1) 1½" x 11"
Dark Blue		
Corners	(4) 3¼" squares	(4) 1⅞" squares

Making Four Corner Squares

1. Cut six yellow squares and two Background squares in half on one diagonal.

12" Block	6" Block
3½" squares	2½" squares

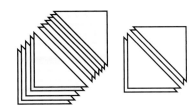

2. Lay out dark blue squares.

12" Block	6" Block
3¼" squares	1⅞" squares

3. Center four Background triangles and four yellow triangles on each side of blue squares.

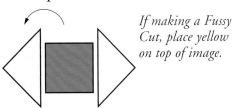

If making a Fussy Cut, place yellow on top of image.

4. Flip square right sides together to triangle. Assembly-line sew with triangle on bottom so bias does not stretch.

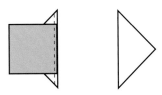

5. Repeat with remaining triangles.

6. Press seams toward triangles. Trim tips.

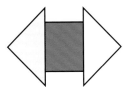 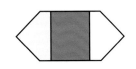

7. Sew Background triangles on remaining sides. Press seams toward triangles.

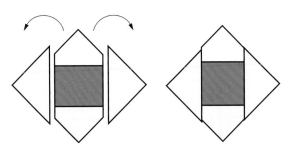

8. Place patches on small cutting mat. Square Corner patches with Fussy Cut Ruler.

12" Block	6" Block
4½" squares	2½" squares

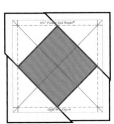
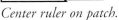
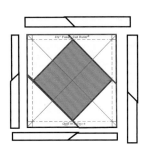

Center ruler on patch.   *Trim on all four sides. Rotate mat as you trim.*

 Making Four Striped Patches

1. Place two strips side by side.

12" Block	6" Block
2½" x 19"	1½" x 11"

2. Flip strip on right together to strip on left, and **sew with scant ¼" seam.**

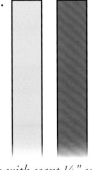

Sew with scant ¼" seam.

3. Set seam with dark fabric on top, open, and press toward dark.

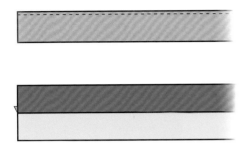

4. Cut into four squares.

12" Block	6" Block
4½" squares	2½" squares

Sewing Block Together

1. **Change back to regular ¼" seam allowance.**

2. Lay out Corners with Striped Patches and Center Square.

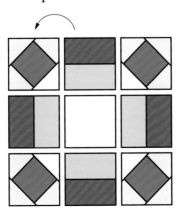

3. Flip middle vertical row to left vertical row, and assembly-line sew. Open. Do not clip connecting threads.

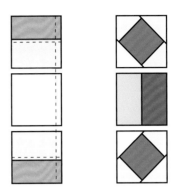

4. Flip right vertical row to middle vertical row, and assembly-line sew. Open. Do not clip connecting threads.

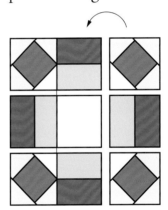

5. Turn. Sew remaining rows, pressing seams away from Corners and toward Stripes.

6. Press just sewn seams toward center.

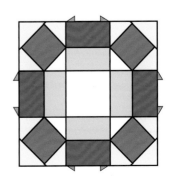

Farmer's Daughter Block

The bright and bold Farmer's Daughter block hangs on the greenhouse of Lora Hurtgom Partyka, fifth generation farmer's daughter, in Kendall, New York. The first generation Hurtgom farm was in Germany. As history evolved, Lora explained that her father remembers, as a young boy of 14, picking up German prisoners of war and driving them to his father's farm to help out in the fields. Working beside her great grandmother and grandmother, Lora recalls packing their home grown vegetables for sale.

The Country Barn Quilt Trail was established in 2006, when Lora erected the first barn quilt at Partyka Farms. With the help of five close friends, they rallied their community in Kendall, NY to create their local quilt trail. In less than three years the Trail has grown to include more than forty barns and other buildings adorned with hand painted quilt squares.

The Farmer's Daughter block was printed in the Kansas City Star in 1932. It was originally pieced with diamonds. To simplify piecing, the diamonds have been replaced with triangle pieced squares. Nancy Cabot referred to the block as Flying Birds. Grandmother Clark named it Jack's Block. Grandma Clark was a name given to a series of booklets from W.L.M. Clark Inc. from St Louis.

photo—Dale Smalley

Skill Level – Easy

....

Supplies

 6" Square Up Ruler
 Marking Pencil

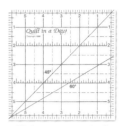

6" Square Up Ruler

	12" Finished Block	**6" Finished Block**
Background		
Rectangles with Points	(1) 2½" x 28" cut into (4) 2½" x 6½"	(1) 1½" x 15" cut into (4) 1½" x 3½"
Framing Border	(2) 1¾" strips cut into (2) 1¾" x 11"	(1) 1¼" strip cut into (2) 1¼" x 6"
Framing Border	(2) 1¾" x 13"	(2) 1¼" x 7"
Green		
Corners and Center	(1) 2½" x 14" strip cut into (5) 2½" squares	(1) 1 ½" x 9" cut into (5) 1½" squares
Yellow		
Nine-Patch	(1) 2½" x 11" cut into (4) 2½" squares	(1) 1½" x 7" cut into (4) 1½" squares
Red		
Nine-Patch and Points	(1) 2½" x 31" cut into (12) 2½" squares	(1) 1½" x 20" cut into (12) 1½" squares

Making Rectangles with Points

1. Turn eight red squares wrong side up.

12" Block	6" Block
2½" squares	1½" squares

2. Draw a diagonal line from corner to corner.

3. Turn four Background Rectangles right side up. Place marked square right sides together to Rectangle.

12" Block	6" Block
2½" x 6½"	1½" x 3½"

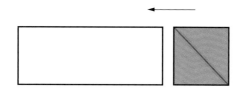

4. Assembly-line sew on right side of line to compensate for fold.

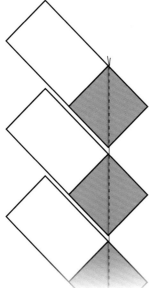

5. Cut apart.

6. Turn Rectangles. Place marked square right sides together to Rectangle.

7. Assembly-line sew on left side of line.

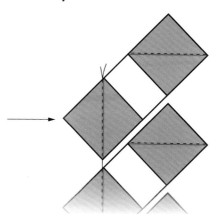

8. Place 6" Square Up Ruler on patch with ¼" lines on sewn lines. Trim ¼" from lines.

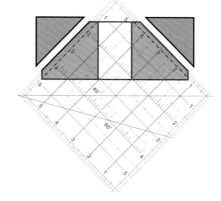

9. Set seams, open, and press toward triangles.

Making Nine-Patch

1. Lay out nine squares for Nine-Patch.

12" Block	6" Block
2½" squares	1½" squares

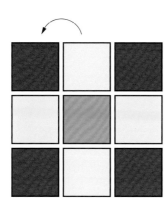

2. Flip middle vertical row onto left vertical row. Assembly-line sew. Do not clip apart.

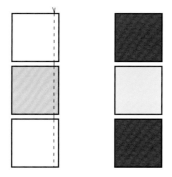

3. Open.

4. Flip right vertical row to middle vertical row. Assembly-line sew. Do not clip apart.

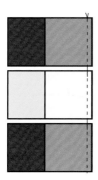

5. Open. Finger press seams toward yellow.

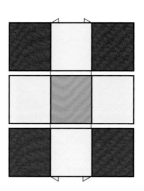

6. Turn.

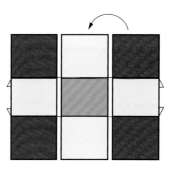

7. Sew remaining rows, pressing seams toward yellow.

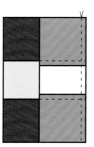

8. Press just sewn seams toward middle row.

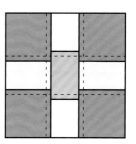

Finishing Block

1. Lay out Nine-Patch, Rectangles with Points, and Corners.

2. Flip middle vertical row onto left vertical row.

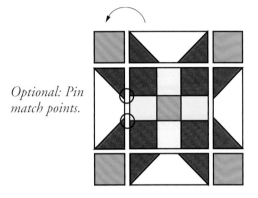

Optional: Pin match points.

3. Assembly-line sew. Do not clip apart.

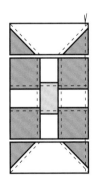

4. Open.

5. Flip right vertical row to middle vertical row.

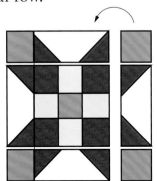

6. Assembly-line sew.

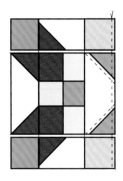

7. Turn. Sew remaining rows, pressing seams away from Rectangles with Points.

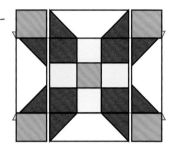

8. Press just sewn seams away from middle.

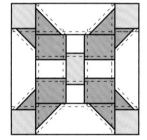

Adding Framing Border

1. Sew strips to two opposite sides with block on top.

12" Block	6" Block
1¾" x 11"	1¼" x 6"

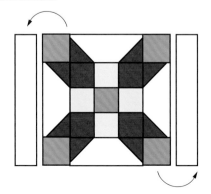

2. Set seams, open, and press toward Border. Trim even with Block.

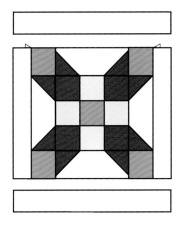

3. Repeat with remaining two sides.

12" Block	6" Block
1¾" x 13"	1¼" x 7"

4. Square block.

12" Block	6" Block
12½" square	6½" square

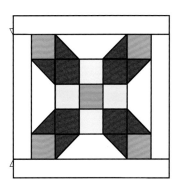

Easy Blackberry Cobbler

Every farmer's daughter knows how to whip up a delicious cobbler from freshly picked blackberries.

½ cup butter, melted
1 cup all-purpose flour
2 cups sugar
3 teaspoons baking powder
pinch salt
1 cup milk
4 cups blackberries
ground cinnamon

Ellie Burns enjoying Grandma's Blackberries – 2008

Preheat oven to 375°.

Place stick of butter in 13" x 9" x 2" baking dish. Melt butter in oven. Cool slightly.

In medium mixing bowl, combine flour, 1 cup sugar, baking powder, and salt, and mix well.

Stir in milk, mixing until just combined. Pour batter over butter but do not stir them together.

Gently stir remaining sugar with blackberries. Pour over top of batter but do not stir them together. Sprinkle cinnamon on top.

Bake in oven approximately 35 to 40 minutes or until top is golden brown. Serve warm or cold with whipped cream or vanilla ice cream.

Farmer's Daughter Quilt

Sue Bouchard designed this charming quilt based on the traditional Farmer's Daughter block. She is actually a daughter of farmers, but was raised a city girl! See photos of her relatives and families' farms on page 216.

The quilt, in popular country hues of green and yellow, is as simple as a John Deere two cylinder tractor, made by reducing the number of parts. It's "built strong" to give you a quilt that will deliver years of trouble free service. Sound familiar?

Sue Bouchard
Amie Potter
52" x 52"

Make nine Farmer's Daughter Blocks

Background	1 yd
	(12) 2½" strips cut into
Rectangles with Points	(36) 2½" x 6½"
Lattice	(24) 2½" x size of Block
Green	**⅔ yd**
	(4) 2½" strips cut into
Corners	(36) 2½" squares
Cornerstones	(16) 2½" squares
Center Nine-Patch	(1) 2½" strip
Border	(3) 2½" strips
Yellow	**⅝ yd**
Center Nine-patch	(4) 2½" strips
Border	(3) 2½" strips
Blue	**1¾ yds**
Center Nine-Patch	(4) 2½" strips
	(5) 2½" strips cut into
Points on Rectangles	(72) 2½" squares
Border	(6) 5½" strips
	(1) 3½" strip cut into
Border Corners	(4) 3½" x 7½"
Binding	**⅝ yd**
	(6) 3" strips
Batting	**60" square**
Backing	**3⅓ yds**

Skill Level – Easy

Supplies

6" Square Up Ruler

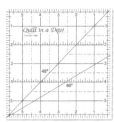

6" Square Up Ruler

Optional

Clearly Perfect Angles
or The Angler 2™

Clearly Perfect Angles

The Angler 2

The purpose of either of these tools is to save time by sewing stitches on the diagonal on unmarked squares. If you don't have one of these tools, draw diagonal lines on 2½" squares for Points with pencil.

The Angler 2 in use

Making Rectangles with Points

1. **Optional:** Read directions for using angle tool included in packaging. The tool is for sewing diagonal lines on unmarked squares.

2. Install tool on sewing machine.

3. Make thirty-six sets of Rectangles with Points. See page 60. Draw diagonal lines on 2½" squares if you don't have a tool.

Making Nine-Patches

Strip sew nine Nine-patches.

1. Sew 2½" strips together.

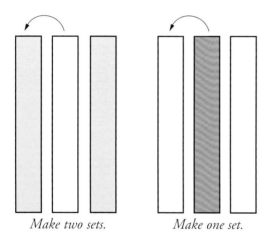

Make two sets.   *Make one set.*

2. Press seams toward yellow.

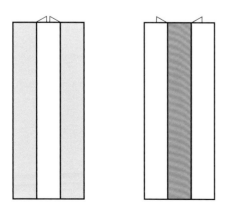

3. Cut into 2½" sections.

4. Sew nine blocks together. Press seams toward yellow.

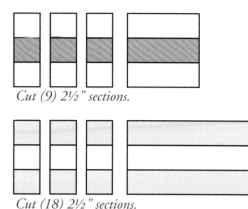

Cut (9) 2½" sections.

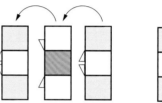

Cut (18) 2½" sections.

5. Press just sewn seams toward yellow.

6. Finish nine blocks following directions on page 62. **Do not add a Framing Border.**

Sewing Top Together

1. Measure size of your block. Cut twenty-four Lattice 2½" x size of your block. Block size should be around 10½".

2. Lay out blocks three across and three down. Place Lattice and 2½" Cornerstones between blocks.

3. Sew top together, pressing seams toward Lattice.

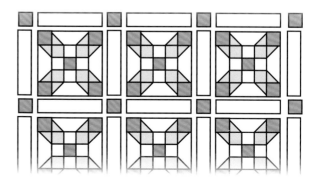

Making Picket Fence Border

1. Sew three 5½" Blue strips to three 2½" Yellow strips. Set seam and press toward Blue.

4. Cut into forty 2½" pairs. **Set four pairs aside.**

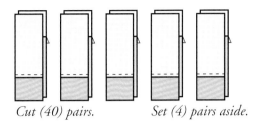

Cut (40) pairs.   *Set (4) pairs aside.*

2. Sew three 5½" Blue strips to three 2½" Green strips. Set seam and press toward Green.

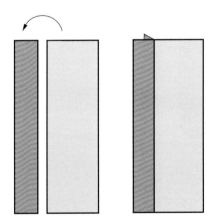

5. Assembly-line sew thirty-six pairs together.

Sew (36) pairs together.

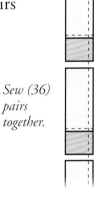

3. With right sides together, layer strip sets with Blue/Green on top.

6. Press seam toward Blue/Yellow.

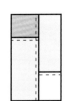

7. Make four rows with nine pairs in each.

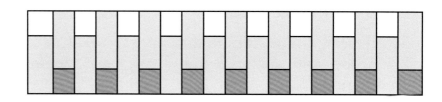

8. From leftover Blue/Green strip, cut four 2½" patches.

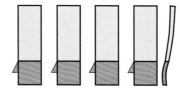

9. Add one patch to the left end of each row. Press seams in same direction. Set two rows aside for Sides.

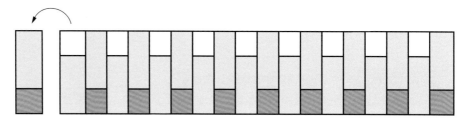

Making Corners for Top and Bottom

1. Take four remaining pairs and stack.

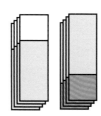

2. Sew 3½" x 7½" Blue to Blue/Yellow. Add the remaining Blue/Green patch on the other side. Press seams toward middle.

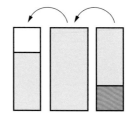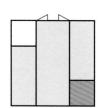

3. Sew one Corner to each end of **top and bottom Border strips**. Seams will lock.

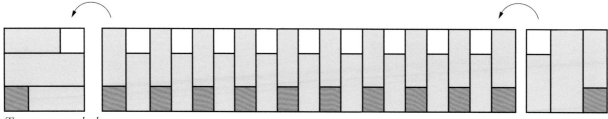

Turn so seams lock.

Supplies
6" Square Up Ruler

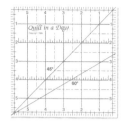

6" Square Up Ruler

	3" Finished Block for 12" Barn	1½" Finished Block for 6" Barn
Blue		
Four-Patches	(1) 1⅛" x 5"	(1) 1" x 4½"
Black		
Four-Patches	(1) 1⅛" x 5"	(1) 1" x 4½"
Yellow		
Four-Patches	(2) 1⅛" x 5"	(2) 1" x 4½"
Background		
Center	(1) 1⅛" square	(1) ¾" square
Red		
Lattice	(4) 1⅛" x 1¾"	(4) ¾" x 1⅛"
Optional Fussy Cut		
"Quilt"	(1) 3½" square	(1) 2" square

The Country Lanes Block has twenty-one pieces in it. The pieces are intricate to sew, especially for the 6" Barn Block with ¼" finished pieces. You may choose to use a Fussy Cut "quilt" instead of a pieced block. See page 21.

71

Miniature Quilt Tips

Making a miniature quilt doesn't mean the project will go faster or be easier. Take your time and be very accurate.

1. Select good quality fabric in **small scale prints** or textures that read solid from a distance. Spray starch and press fabrics.

2. Carefully cut pieces using accurate rulers and sharp rotary cutter. Cutting pieces oversized and cutting them back to designated size after sewing also works well.

3. Put a fresh #70 needle in your sewing machine. A slightly bent needle will ruin your work.

4. Use a stiletto to pick up pieces, and hold pieces in place while you sew. A hands free magnifying glass is useful. Proper lighting is also important.

5. Press sewn pieces after every step. Be careful of distortion. Check accuracy of work against given measurements. If you are even a thread off, imperfect work will show.

6. Trim scant ¼" seams back to ⅛" so pieces do not overlap after they are pressed open.

Changing the seam width by one thread makes a difference. All these blocks were made trying to achieve the perfect sizes for the barns.

Eleanor Burns
11" x 15"

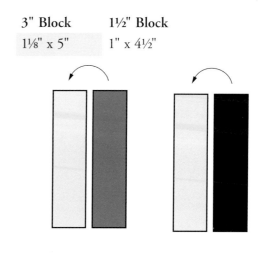 Making Four-Patches

1. Sew with **scant ¼" seam**.

2. Lay out blue and yellow strips for first set and black and yellow strips for second set.

3" Block	1½" Block
1⅛" x 5"	1" x 4½"

3. Flip right sides together, and assembly-line sew.

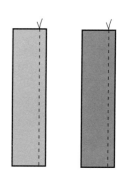

4. Press seams away from yellow.

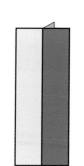 

5. Place yellow/blue strip right side up, with yellow across top. Place yellow/black strip right sides together to yellow/blue strip, locking seams.

6. Straighten left edge. Layer cut strip sets into four segments.

3" Block	1½" Block
1⅛" segments	¾" segments

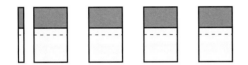

7. Assembly-line sew four pairs together.

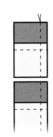

8. Open block and lay flat, wrong side up. Push top vertical seam to right, and bottom vertical seam to left. Centers pop open. "Swirl" seams around center, and press.

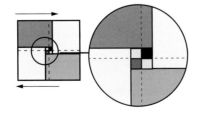

9. Square Four-Patches.

3" Block	1½" Block
1¾" square	1" - 1 1/16" square

Sewing Block Together

1. Lay out Lattice with Four-Patches and Center. Flip middle vertical row to left, right sides together.

3" Block	1½" Block
1⅛" x 1¾"	¾" x 1⅛"
1⅛" square	¾" square

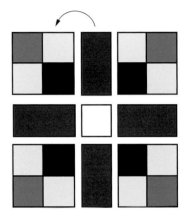

2. Assembly-line sew. Open.

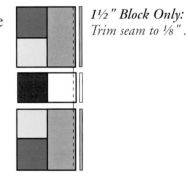

1½" Block Only: Trim seam to ⅛".

3. Finger press seams toward Lattice.

4. Open. Flip right row to middle row right sides together, and assembly-line sew. **1½" Block Only:** Trim seam to ⅛".

5. Open, and turn. Sew remaining rows, locking and pressing seams toward Lattice.

6. From wrong side, press just sewn seams toward center.

7. Square block.

3" Block	1½" Block
3½" square	2" square

Gothic Barn

Eleanor Burns stitched up this "fun" Gothic Barn painted with polka dots just for "Happy the Pig" as he stretches out on green checked grass.

Teresa Varnes plopped a lazy old cow outside her wooden front door set into brick. She used a tiny zig-zag to simulate the roof on the upper level.

Chris Levine selected fabric woven with a stripe for her top level in place of stitching lines. The plank door is also fabric as well as the bricks. Note the satin stitching for the outside of the windows, and straight stitching on the inside. A contented kitty sleeps outside the door!

Gothic Barns feature a unique curved roof, which is the signature of the building. The lower level is usually concrete masonry with a large open space in the interior for a milking parlor. The upper level is usually wood with increased interior storage capacity for hay and an overhead conveyor.

Skill Level – Easy

Supplies
  Off-white Machine thread
  Black Machine thread
  Marking Pencil for Black fabric
  Point Turner

Point Turner

	12" Finished Barn	6" Finished Barn
Background or Wood Grain		
Top Roof	(1) 3" x 10"	(1) 2" x 5"
Center Roof	(2) 3½" x 5"	(2) 2" x 2⅝"
Bottom Roof	(1) 2½" x 13"	(1) 1¼" x 7"
Brown Wood Grain		
Door	(1) 3" x 2"	(1) 2" x 1½"
Black		
Windows	(1) 3" square	(1) 2" square
Brick		
Sides of Door	(2) 3" x 5⅞"	(2) 2" x 3"
Top of Door	(1) 1½" x 12¾"	(1) 1" x 6¾"
Directional Sky		
Sky	(1) 8" x 13"	(1) 4½" x 7"
Green		
Ground	(1) 2" x 12¾"	(1) 1" x 6¾"
Non-woven Fusible Interfacing		
Roof	(1) 8" x 13"	(1) 4¼" x 7"
Paper Backed Fusible Web		
Windows	(1) 2¾" square	(1) 1¾" square

Making Gothic Roof

1. Lay out Country Lanes block with Center Roof rectangles. Sew block to each side of rectangles.

12" Barn	6" Barn
3½" x 5"	2" x 2⅝"

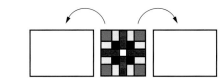

If necessary, trim rectangles to size of block.

2. Press seams away from block.

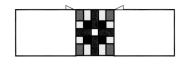

3. Center Top and Bottom rows with block row, and sew together.

12" Barn	6" Barn
3" x 10"	2" x 5"
2½" x 13"	1¼" x 7"

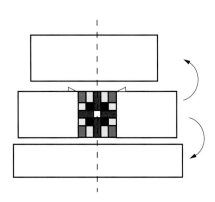

4. Press seams away from block row.

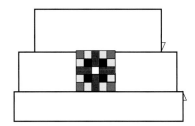

Sewing Wood Grain *(Optional)*

If you did not use wood grain fabric, sew lines on Roof.

1. Place black thread on top and in bobbin.

2. Mark equally spaced lines between two seams with Hera Marker or disappearing marker.

3. Stitch with 3.0 stitch length on seam lines above and below quilt block.

12" Barn	6" Barn
Approximately ½" apart	Approximately ¼" apart

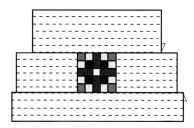

You can also use your sewing machine foot to sew equally spaced lines.

4. Continue sewing equally spaced lines to outside edges.

Sewing Interfacing to Roof

1. Place non-woven fusible interfacing with smooth side up on Roof pattern.

12" Barn	6" Barn
8" x 13"	4¼" x 7"

2. Trace appropriate size Roof pattern with permanent marking pen. Mark centers.

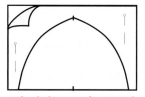

Black line is for 12" barn.

3. Place fusible side of interfacing against pieced Roof. Line up center line with center of block. Pin.

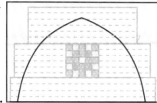

4. Place metal open toe foot on sewing machine. Lighten pressure on presser foot. Sew on curved line with 18 stitches per inch. Pivot with needle down at peak of Roof.

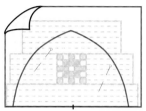

Sew on curved line. Pivot at peak

5. Return machine to regular setting.

6. Trim ⅛" from line.

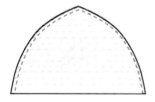

7. Turn right side out. Push out curves and peak with point turner.

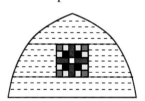

8. Center Roof on Sky, and match up bottom edges. Fuse in place with hot steam iron.

12" Barn	6" Barn
8" x 13"	4½" x 7"

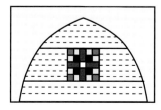

Sewing Door

1. Place Door between two Side patches and sew.

12" Barn	6" Barn
3" x 2"	2" x 1½"
3" x 5⅞"	2" x 3"

2. Press seams toward Door.

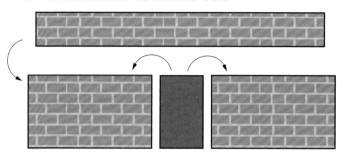

3. Sew Top Row of bricks to Door.

12" Barn	6" Barn
1½" x 12¾"	1" x 6¾"

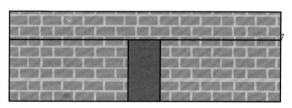

4. Press seam toward top.

Cutting Two Windows

1. Turn Window fabric wrong side up.

12" Barn	6" Barn
3" square	2" square

2. Center paper backed fusible web on Window fabric with fusible side against wrong side.

3. Fuse in place for two seconds.

4. Cut out two Windows.

12" Barn	6" Barn
1⅛" x 1¼"	⅝" x 1"

5. Peel paper away.

6. Place Windows to left and right of Door with fusible side of Window against right side of brick fabric.

12" Barn	6" Barn
2" from Door	¾" from Door

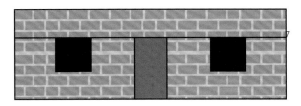

7. Fuse in place for ten seconds.

Finishing Two Windows

1. Mark a lengthwise sewing line through center of Window.

2. Mark two vertical lines equally spaced from ends.

 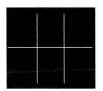

3. Place off-white thread on top of machine and in bobbin.

4. Satin stitch on marked lines.

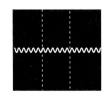

5. Satin stitch around outside edge of Window. Pivot at corners with needle down on outside edge.

Setting a Satin Stitch

1. Select satin stitch *(zig-zag stitch)* on your sewing machine.

2. Set stitch width at approximately 3.0 and stitch length at 0.3.

3. Place open toe appliqué foot on sewing machine.

4. Practice stitch on scrap fabric. Place stabilizer under fabric if it puckers.

Satin Stitch Roof Line

1. Place black thread on top and in bobbin.

2. Set zig-zag stitch width at approximately 5.0 and stitch length at 0.3.

3. Zig-zag around Roof, anchoring Roof to Sky and giving Roof a finished look.

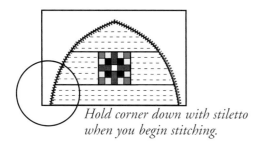

Hold corner down with stiletto when you begin stitching.

Finishing Barn

1. Lay out Roof with Door/ Windows and Ground.

2. Sew together.

3. Press seams away from middle section.

4. Square Barn.

12" Barn	6" Barn
12½" square	6½" square

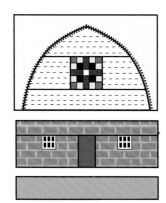 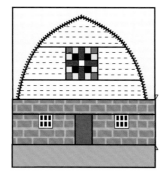

Gathering Eggs

In 1959 when I was 8, we were visiting Grandpa and Grandma on their farm in Nebraska. I pestered Grandma to allow me to go gather the eggs in the hen house. She relented and gave me a wire egg basket to collect the eggs. When I entered the hen house, I discovered that I was afraid of the chickens – they pecked! So my grand plan was to gather the eggs from the roosts where the hen was absent! Unfortunately, there weren't very many and when I took my meager collection into Grandma, she asked me if that is all there were. "Yup, that's all there were", I replied. I know she went back out later and really collected the eggs while I was occupied elsewhere.

Linda Parker, Farm of Casper Meirose, Hartington, Nebraska

Quatrefoil Block

In the dictionary, quatrefoil is a stylized representation of a flower with four petals or of a leaf with four leaflets. Nancy Cabot, pen name for Loretta Leitner Rising of the Chicago Tribune, named the quilt block in the 1930's.

Clover is a trefoil, having leaves with three leaflets. However, clovers occasionally have leaves with four leaflets, becoming a quatrefoil. These four leaf clovers, like other rarities, are considered lucky. A common saying is "to be in clover", meaning to be living a carefree life of ease, comfort, or prosperity. This stems from the historical use of clover as "green manure" planted after harvesting a crop. A farmer whose fields were "in the clover" was finished for the season.

photo –Brian Sceutel

The big red barn belonging to Keith and Shelli Berry, Sac City, Iowa, has been in the family since 1961. The barn features a gambrel roof with cupola, lightning rods, and weather vane. If you drive past the Berry barn, you will see their State Fair quilt pattern, which Art Director Merritt Voigtlander replaced with Photoshop for lack of a Quatrefoil block on a beautiful barn.

Supplies

Mini Geese Ruler One

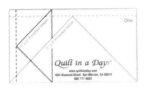

Mini Geese Ruler One

		12" Finished Block	6" Finished Block
Background			
	Four-Patch	(2) 2½" x 11"	(2) 1½" x 7"
	Center	(1) 4½" square	(1) 2½" square
	Geese	(1) 7" square	(1) 5" square
Yellow			
	Four-Patch	(1) 2½" x 11"	(1) 1½" x 7"
Green			
	Four-Patch	(1) 2½" x 11"	(1) 1½" x 7"
	Rectangles	(4) 2½" x 4½"	(4) 1½" x 2½"
	Geese	(1) 5½" square	(1) 3½" square

Making Four-Patches

Follow pressing instructions closely so seams lock together.

1. Lay out two Background strips. Place a yellow strip and a green strip with each Background strip.

12" Block	6" Block
2½" x 11"	1½" x 7"

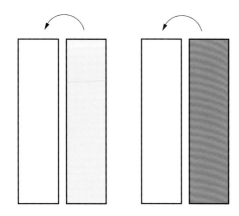

2. Flip right sides together, and assembly-line sew.

3. Place on pressing mat with Background on top. Set seams.

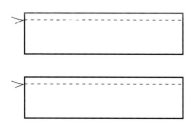

4. Open and press toward Background.

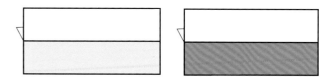

5. Place pieces right sides together with yellow on top.

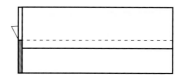

6. Layer cut into four pieces.

12" Block	6" Block
2½" pieces	1½" pieces

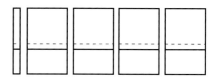

7. Assembly-line sew, locking center seams.

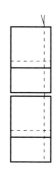

8. Set seam with green/Background on top.

9. Open and press seam toward green/Background.

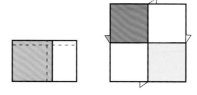

Making Geese

1. Place Background square right side up. Center Geese square on Background square, right sides together.

12" Block
5½" square
7" square

6" Block
3½" square
5" square

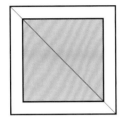

2. Draw diagonal line corner to corner.

3. Follow Geese instructions beginning on page 26.

4. Square using Mini Geese Ruler One.

12" Finished Block	**6" Finished Block**
Square to 2" x 4" Finished Size or 2½" x 4½" including seams	Square to 1" x 2" Finished Size or 1½" x 2½" including seams

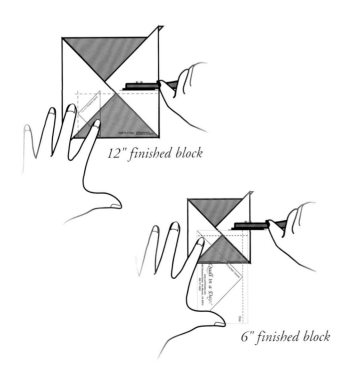

12" finished block

6" finished block

 Sewing Rectangles to Geese

1. Place four rectangles with Geese.

12" Block
2½" x 4½"

6" Block
1½" x 2½"

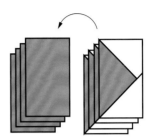

2. Assembly-line sew. Clip apart.

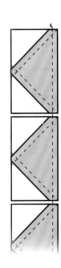

3. Place on pressing mat with **rectangles on top.**

4. Set seams, open, and press.

Set seam.   *Seams are pressed toward rectangles.*

Sewing Block Together

1. Lay out block following seam placements. Seams will lock.

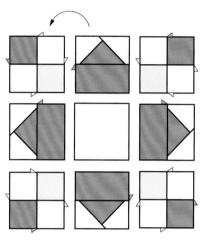

2. Flip middle vertical row to left vertical row, and assembly-line sew. Open.

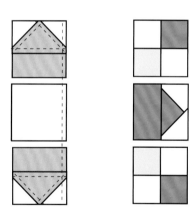

3. Flip right vertical row to middle vertical row, and assembly-line sew. Open.

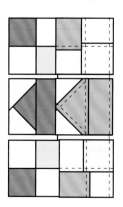

4. Turn. Sew remaining rows, pressing seams away from rectangles.

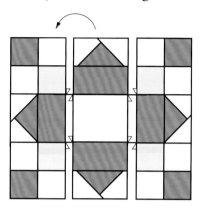

5. Press just sewn seams away from center.

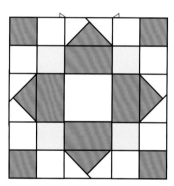

6. Measure block.

12" Block	6" Block
12½"	6½"

Our Favorite Cow

We had a little black Angus cow named Pixie. She was very gentle, and contrary to my dad's rule of all animals earning their keep, Pixie became a pet and lived on the farm for many years. Pixie loved peanut butter and jelly sandwiches. When it came time to move the stock (usually about 8-10 head) from one pasture to another, Mom would make a supply of sandwiches. Daddy would get a flatbed trailer hitched to the Farmall tractor. My little sister and I would ride on the trailer, feeding sandwiches to Pixie as we rolled slowly along. The trick was making the sandwiches last long enough. As Pixie plodded along behind the tractor, reaching her neck out to take bites of the sandwiches, the other cattle would follow her! The process worked very smoothly every single time! One time though, Mom forgot she had put a peanut butter and jelly sandwich in her pocket to give to my dad who was working out in the field. She stopped in the pasture to say hi to Pixie. Pixie smelled that sandwich and before Mom realized what was going on, Pixie had torn the pocket right off Mom's apron and had that entire sandwich in her mouth, happily munching away! Laughing, Mom went back into the house to make Daddy another sandwich and this time, bypassed the cow on her way to deliver his lunch!

Mary Zawlocki

Cups and Saucers Block

The Cups and Saucers block is prominently displayed on the gable end of the barn owned by Ralph and Virginia Trecartin in Kendall, New York. When the Country Barn Quilt Trail was established in 2006, participants were encouraged to select a quilt pattern with meaning. The couple selected Cups and Saucers to honor Virginia's Australian mother, Elizabeth Schumacher Bourne, and grandmother, who often shared tea in their native home. The beautiful bright yellow in the block is a loving tribute to her mother's sunny disposition. Cups and Saucers is a Kansas City Star pattern printed in 1936.
www.countrybarnquilttrail.com

Elizabeth Schumacher Bourne on the day of her engagement

photo – Dale Smalley

Elizabeth in later years

Skill Level – Easy

....

Supplies

Mini Geese Ruler One
6½" Triangle Square Up Ruler

Mini Geese Ruler One

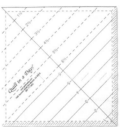

6½" Triangle Square Up Ruler

	12" Finished Block	6" Finished Block
Blue		
Corners	(1) 5" x 10"	(1) 3" x 6"
Green		
Corners	(1) 5" x 10"	(1) 3" x 6"
Red		
Geese	(1) 5½" square	(1) 3½" square
Center	(1) 4½" square	(1) 2½" square
Black		
Geese	(1) 5½" square	(1) 3 ½" square
Yellow		
Geese	(2) 7" squares	(2) 5" squares

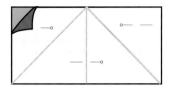

Making Four Corners

1. Place two fabrics right sides together.

12" Block	6" Block
5" x 10"	3" x 6"

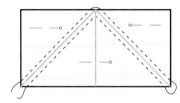

2. Draw a center line.

3. Draw diagonal lines. Pin.

4. Sew a ¼" seam on both sides of diagonal lines. Remove Pins. Press.

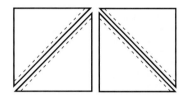

5. Cut apart on marked lines.

6. Square with 6½" Triangle Square Up Ruler.

12" Block	6" Block
4½" square	2½" square

12" Block

Place 4½" red dashed line on 6½" Triangle Square Up Ruler **on stitching line**. Center ruler on patch. Trim two sides.

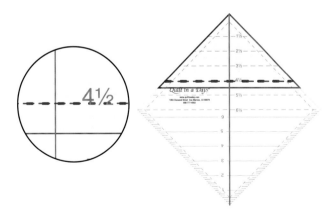

6" Block

Place 2½" red dashed line on 6½" Triangle Square Up Ruler **on stitching line**. Center ruler on patch. Trim two sides.

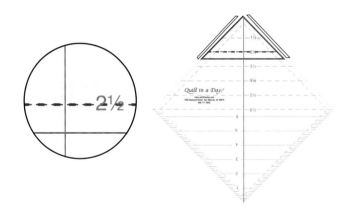

7. Set seam with dark fabric on top.

8. Open, and press seams toward dark.

9. Trim tips.

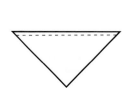
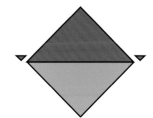

Making Geese

Use Mini Geese Ruler One.

1. Place red and black squares right sides together and centered on yellow squares.

12" Block	6" Block
5½" squares	3½" squares
7" squares	5" squares

2. Draw diagonal lines corner to corner.

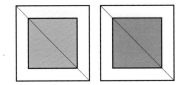

3. Follow Geese instructions beginning on page 26.

4. Square up using Mini Geese Ruler One.

12" Finished Block	6" Finished Block
Square to 2" x 4" Finished Size or 2½" x 4½" including seams	Square to 1" x 2" Finished Size or 1½" x 2½" including seams

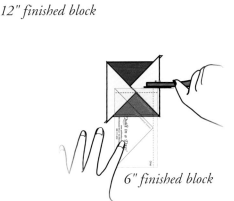

12" finished block

6" finished block

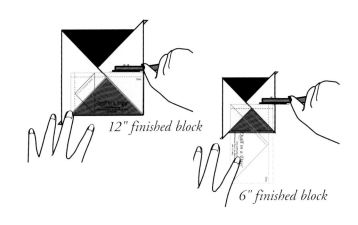

12" finished block

6" finished block

Sewing Geese Together

1. Lay out two stacks of Geese with four in each stack.

2. Flip geese on right to Geese on left, right sides together.

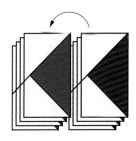

3. Assembly-line sew.

4. Set seam with red Geese on top, open, and press toward red Geese.

Finishing Block

1. Lay out Geese patches with Center and Corners.

12" Block	6" Block
4½" squares	2½" squares

2. Flip middle vertical row right sides together to vertical row on left.

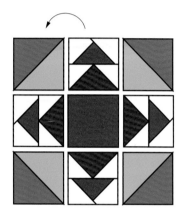

3. Assembly-line sew. **Do not clip connecting threads.**

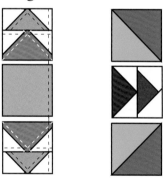

4. Open. Flip right vertical row to middle vertical row.

5. Assembly-line sew. **Do not clip connecting threads.**

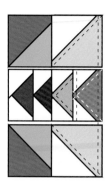

6. Turn.

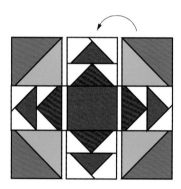

7. Sew remaining rows, pressing seams away from geese.

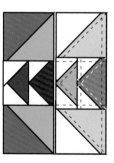

8. Press just sewn seams away from center.

My Pet Lamb

When I was about 5 years old, I had a pet lamb named Susie. (Yes, Mary really did have a little lamb!) Susie followed me everywhere, just like a little dog. I loved her and she loved me. One day, the bookmobile was coming for it's monthly visit. I was so excited. I'd recently learned to write my name so I could get a library card. I wanted to go, but I couldn't leave Susie at home! Mama helped me give Susie a bath so she smelled nice and clean. Then I painted her toenails a pretty pink (I painted mine too!) and tied a pretty silky scarf around her neck. Finally, I dressed up in my bride's costume that my mom had made for me, veil and all! I was finally ready for the bookmobile!

When it came into view and rolled to a stop, the doors slid open with a whoosh of air and scent of books. I had a light rope on Susie's neck and I led her up the steps and down the wide aisle of the bus. The driver and the library ladies all oohed and awed at such a pretty lamb and her bride! We set Susie up on the shelf in the back window where she waited patiently for me to choose my books. Everyone was dutifully impressed with the pair of us! I was so proud! When it came time to leave, Mama set Susie back down on the floor and we all clomped our way back up the aisle and down the steps of the bookmobile, waving to everyone as we left. The smiles I saw that day are a huge part of that fond memory!

Mary Zawlocki

Corn and Beans Block

According to Iroquois legend, corn, beans, and squash are three inseparable sisters who only grow and thrive together. They are known as The Three Sisters. Corn provides a natural pole for bean vines to climb. Beans fix nitrogen on their roots, improving the overall fertility of the plot by providing nitrogen to the following years' corn. Bean vines also help stabilize the corn plants, making them less vulnerable to blowing over in the wind. Shallow-rooted squash vines become a living mulch, shading emerging weeds and preventing soil moisture from evaporating. Spiny squash plants also help discourage predators from approaching the corn and beans. The crop residue is added back into the mound at the end of the season.

Jason and Lisa Paysen's barn, Sac City, IA, still has the original wood barn board and batten siding and a salt box roof. Originally used for livestock, it's now used for storage. Notice the lightning rods on the roof.

The Corn and Beans pattern was published by the Ladies Art Company prior to 1895. It was their 100th quilt pattern.

photo –John Zeman www.barnquilts.com

Skill Level – Intermediate

Supplies

Mini Geese Ruler One
6½" Triangle Square Up Ruler
6" x 12" Ruler

Mini Geese Ruler One

6½" Triangle Square Up Ruler

	12" Finished Block	6" Finished Block
Background		
Geese	(1) 7" square	(1) 5" square
Corners	(2) 5⅛" squares	(2) 3" squares
Large Rectangle	(1) 4½" x 5½"	(1) 2½" x 3½"
Corn	(1) 3" x 6"	(1) 2" x 4"
Corn Rectangle	(4) 2½" x 3½"	(4) 1½" x 2½"
Green		
Large Rectangle	(1) 4½" x 5½"	(1) 2½" x 3½"
Geese	(1) 5½" square	(1) 3½" square
Yellow		
Corn	(4) 3" squares	(4) 1⅞" squares
Corn	(1) 3" x 6"	(1) 2" x 4"

Making Corn

1. Place Background and Corn right sides together. Draw a center line.

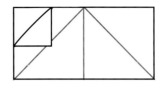

2. Draw diagonal lines.

12" Block	6" Block
3" x 6"	2" x 4"

3. Sew ¼" seam on both sides of diagonal lines.

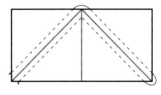

4. Cut apart on all lines.

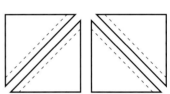

5. Square patches with 6½" Triangle Square Up Ruler.

12" Block	6" Block
2½" square	1½" square

12" Block

Place 2½" red dashed line on 6½" Triangle Square Up Ruler **on stitching line**. Center ruler on patch. Trim two sides.

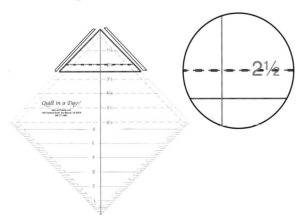

6" Block

Place 1½" red dashed line on 6½" Triangle Square Up Ruler **on stitching line**. Center ruler on patch. Trim two sides.

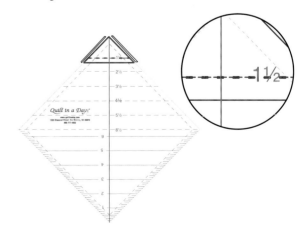

6. Set seam with Corn on top, open, and press toward Corn.

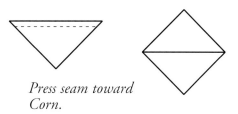

Press seam toward Corn.

7. Lay out four Corn pointing downward with Background rectangles.

12" Block	6" Block
2½" x 3½"	1½" x 2½"

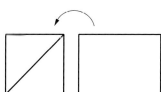

8. Flip Background right sides together to Corn, and assembly-line sew.

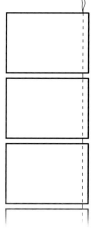

9. Press seam toward Background.

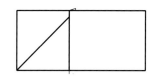

10. Make two stacks of two each. Flip pieces right sides together.

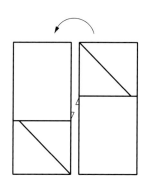

11. Assembly-line sew.

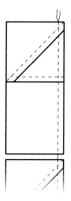

12. Fold in half, and clip seam to the stitching.

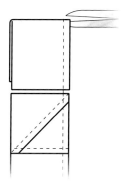

13. Open. Press, pushing clipped seam to rectangles.

14. Measure patch.

12" Block	6" Block
4½" x 5½"	2½" x 3½"

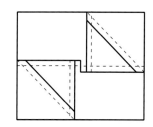

Diagonal line

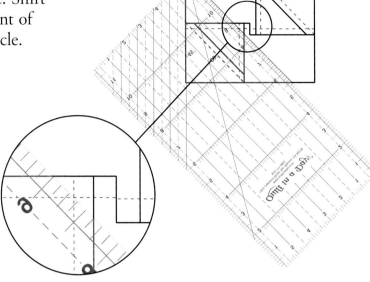

15. Turn patch wrong side up. Lay diagonal line on 6" x 12" ruler on short side. Shift ruler until ruler's edge is at the point of the Triangle Pieced Square. See circle.

16. Draw a pencil line that is your **sewing line.**

17. Turn patch, and draw another sewing line across point of other Triangle Pieced Square.

18. The distance between the parallel lines is about ½", or two seam allowances.

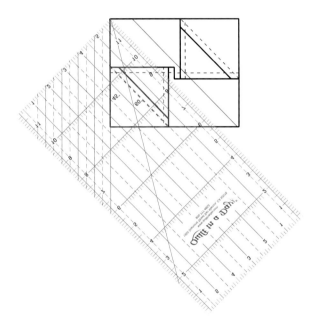

19. Place patches right sides together with one Background Large Rectangle and one Beans Large Rectangle. Pin.

12" Block	6" Block
4½" x 5½"	2½" x 3½"

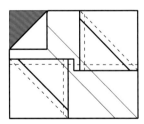

20. Assembly-line sew on lines.

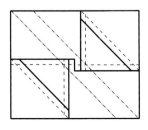

21. Cut between lines.

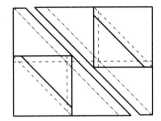

22. Set seams with Large Triangle on top.

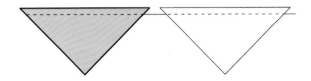

23. Open, and press seam toward Large Triangle.

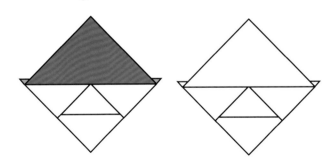

24. Measure patch. Sliver trim if necessary. Trim tips.

12" Block	6" Block
4½" square	2½" square

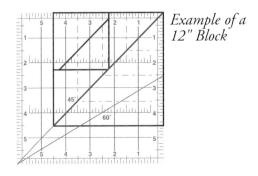

Example of a 12" Block

Sewing Center Together

1. Lay out four patches.

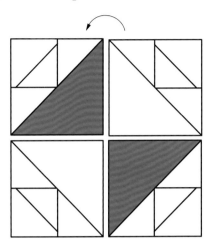

2. Flip right sides together. Assembly-line sew, being careful not to cut off points.

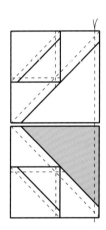

3. Turn. Sew remaining row, pushing top seam up and underneath seam down.

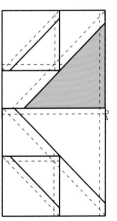

Push top seam up and underneath seam down.

4. Clip connecting thread, and "swirl" seams around center.

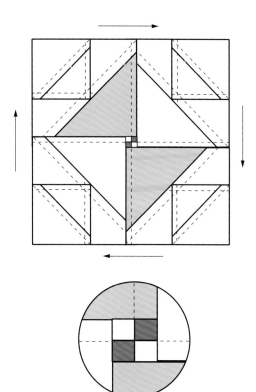

 Making Four Geese

Use Mini Geese Ruler One for 2" x 4" finished Geese for 12" Block and 1" x 2" finished Geese for 6" Block.

1. Place green square right sides together and centered on Background square.

12" Block	6" Block
5½" square	3½" square
7" square	5" square

2. Draw diagonal line corner to corner.

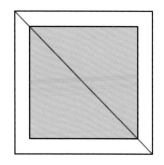

3. Follow Geese instructions beginning on page 26.

4. Square using Mini Geese Ruler One.

12" Finished Block	6" Finished Block
Square to 2" x 4" Finished Size or 2½" x 4½" including seams	Square to 1" x 2" Finished Size or 1½" x 2½" including seams

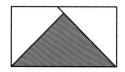

5. Cut four yellow squares on one diagonal.

12" Block	6" Block
3" squares	1⅞" squares

6. Stack triangles with Geese. Flip Geese to left triangle, and assembly-line sew.

7. Flip right triangle to Geese, and assembly-line sew.

8. Press seams toward triangles. Trim tips.

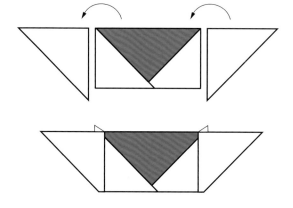

Finishing Block

1. Lay out Geese with center patch.

2. Sew Geese to two opposite sides of center, locking seams.

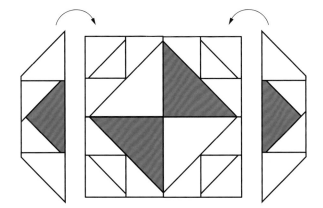

3. Press seams toward Geese. Trim tips.

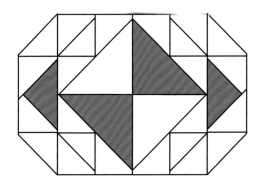

4. Repeat on remaining two sides.

5. Cut two Background squares in half on one diagonal.

12" Block	6" Block
5⅛" squares	3" squares

6. Center and sew triangles to corners of block, with triangles on bottom so bias does not stretch.

Check for ¼" seam. Trim if necessary.

7. Set seams, open, and press seams toward triangles.

8. Square block.

12" Block	6" Block
12½" square	6½" square

99

Hens and Chicks Block

Randell and Dorothy Kreft have owned the barn, built in 1949, in Sac City, Iowa since 1960. The original horizontal wood siding remains on the structure and the gothic roof is covered with asphalt shingles. The roof features a cupola and lightning rods.

Carlie Sexton Holmes, who ran a mail order pattern company from Wheaton, Ill, named the block Wild Goose Chase in 1928. Along those same lines, Nancy Cabot, pen name for Loretta Leitner Rising, named the block Fox and Geese in 1933 and published it in the Chicago Tribune. Ruth Finley named the block Ducks and Ducklings. She wrote *Old Patchwork Quilts and the Women Who Made Them* in 1929, which was a popular book at that time.

photo –Brian Steutel

Skill Level – Easy

....

Supplies

6½" Triangle Square
Up Ruler
6" x 12" Ruler

*6½" Triangle Square
Up Ruler*

6" x 12" Ruler

	12" Finished Block	6" Finished Block
Yellow		
Chicks	(1) 3½" x 7"	(1) 2¼" x 4½"
Chicks Rectangle	(4) 2⅞" x 4"	(4) 1¾" x 2½"
Lattice	(4) 3⅛" x 5¼"	(4) 1½" x 3"
Red		
Chicks	(1) 3½" x 7"	(1) 2¼" x 4½"
Green		
Hens	(2) 5¼" x 6⅜"	(2) 3" x 3¾"
Brown		
Center Square	(1) 3⅛" square	(1) 1½" square

Making Chicks

1. Place yellow and Chicks right sides together. Draw a center line.

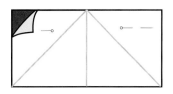

2. Draw diagonal lines.

12" Block	6" Block
3½" x 7"	2¼" x 4½"

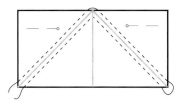

3. Sew ¼" seam on both sides of diagonal lines.

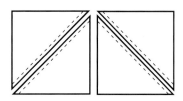

4. Cut apart on all lines.

5. Square patches with 6½" Triangle Square Up Ruler.

12" Block	6" Block
2⅞" square	1¾" square

12" Block

Place 2⅞" green solid lines found on sides of 6½" Triangle Square Up Ruler **on stitching line**. Center ruler on patch. Trim two sides.

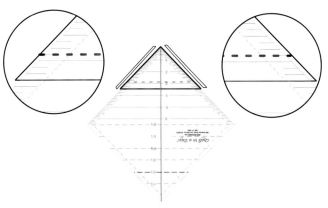

6" Block

Place 1¾" red solid lines found on sides of 6½" Triangle Square Up Ruler **on stitching line**. Center ruler on patch. Trim two sides.

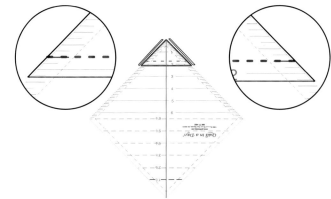

6. Set seam with Chicks on top, open, and press toward Chicks.

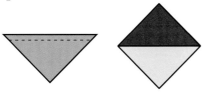

Press seam toward Chicks.

7. Lay out four Chicks pointing downward with yellow rectangles.

12" Block	6" Block
2⅞" x 4"	1¾" x 2½"

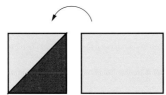

8. Flip yellow right sides together to Chicks, and assembly-line sew.

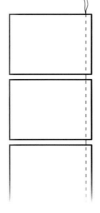

9. Press seam toward yellow.

10. Make two stacks of two each. Flip pieces right sides together.

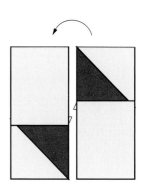

11. Assembly-line sew.

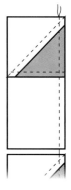

12. Fold in half, and clip seam to the stitching.

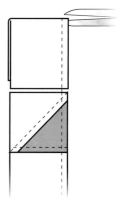

13. Open. Press, pushing clipped seam to rectangles.

14. Measure patch.

12" Block	6" Block
5½" x 6⅜"	3" x 3¾"

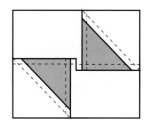

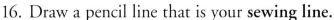

Diagonal line

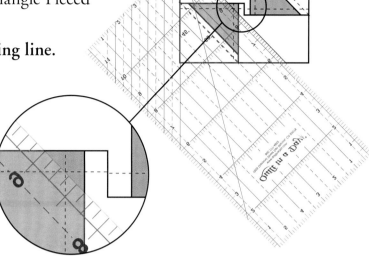

15. Turn patch wrong side up. Lay diagonal line on 6" x 12" ruler on short side. Shift ruler until ruler's edge is at the point of the Triangle Pieced Square. See circle.

16. Draw a pencil line that is your **sewing line.**

17. Turn patch, and draw another sewing line across point of other Triangle Pieced Square.

18. The distance between the parallel lines is about ½", or two seam allowances.

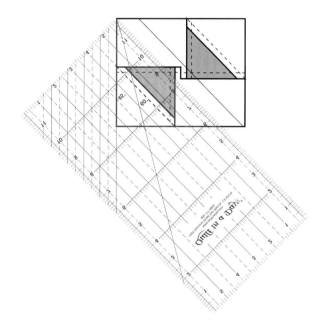

19. Place patches right sides together with Hens rectangle. Pin.

12" Block	6" Block
5¼" x 6⅜"	3" x 3¾"

20. Assembly-line sew on lines.

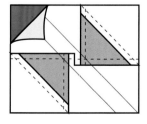
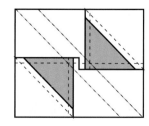

21. Cut between lines.

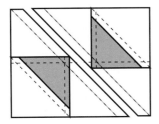

22. Set seams with Hens triangle on top.

23. Open, and press seam toward Hens.

24. Measure patch. Sliver trim if necessary. Trim tips.

12" Block	6" Block
5¼" square	3" square

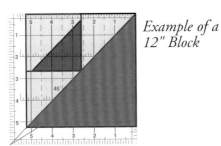

Example of a 12" Block

 Sewing Block Together

1. Lay out four patches with Lattice and Center Square.

12" Block	6" Block
3⅛" x 5¼"	1½" x 3"
3⅛" square	1½" square

2. Flip right sides together. Assembly-line sew vertical rows.

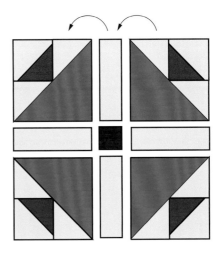

3. Turn. Sew remaining rows, pushing seams toward Lattice.

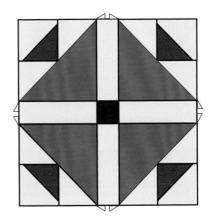

4. Press last seams toward center.

Gambrel Roof Barn
with Flying Geese Block

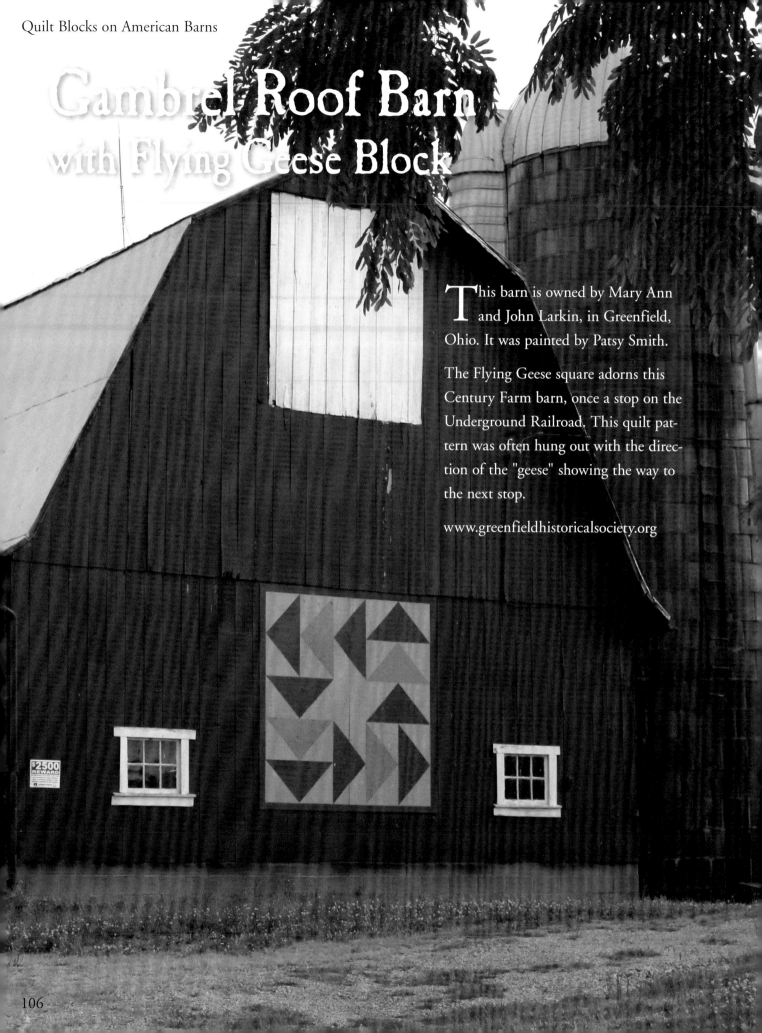

This barn is owned by Mary Ann and John Larkin, in Greenfield, Ohio. It was painted by Patsy Smith.

The Flying Geese square adorns this Century Farm barn, once a stop on the Underground Railroad. This quilt pattern was often hung out with the direction of the "geese" showing the way to the next stop.

www.greenfieldhistoricalsociety.org

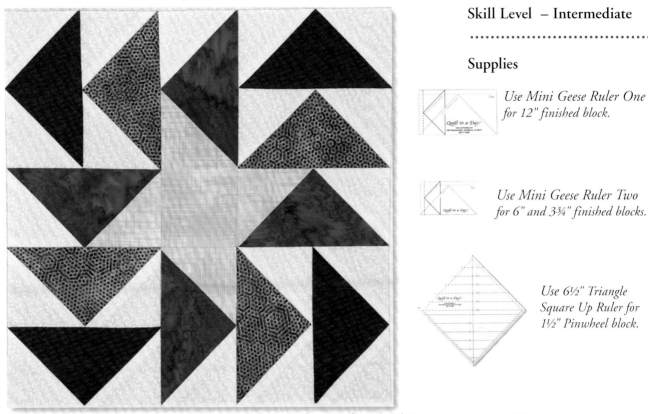

Supplies

Use Mini Geese Ruler One for 12" finished block.

Use Mini Geese Ruler Two for 6" and 3¾" finished blocks.

Use 6½" Triangle Square Up Ruler for 1½" Pinwheel block.

Make a 1½" finished size Pinwheel block for 6" finished Barn on page 111.

	12" Finished Block	6" Finished Block	3¾" Finished Block For Block on 12" Barn
Background			
Framing Border	(2) 1¾" strips cut into (2) 1¾" x 11" (2) 1¾" x 13"	(1) 1¾" strip cut into (2) 1¾" x 5" (2) 1¾" x 7"	
Geese	(3) 7" squares	(3) 4½" squares	(3) 4½" squares
Yellow			
Geese	(1) 7" square	(1) 4½" square	(1) 4½" square
Center	(1) 2½" square	(1) 1¼" square	(1) 1¼" square
Red			
Geese	(1) 5½" square	(1) 3" square	(1) 3" square
Green			
Geese	(1) 5½" square	(1) 3" square	(1) 3" square
Blue			
Geese	(2) 5½" squares	(2) 3" squares	(2) 3" squares

Making Red Geese and Green Geese

1. Place one red square right sides together and centered on one Background square.

2. Repeat with one green square and one Background square.

12" Block	6" and 3¾" Blocks
5½" and 7"	3" and 4½"

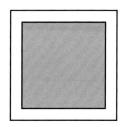 

3. Draw diagonal line corner to corner on both sets of squares. Sew ¼" from both sides of drawn line. Cut on drawn line.

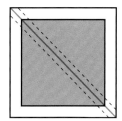 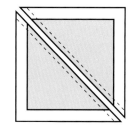

4. Follow Geese directions beginning on page 26.

5. Square four red Geese and four green Geese.

12" Block

Use green lines on Mini Geese Ruler One. Square to 2" x 4" Finished Size or 2½" x 4½" including seams.

6" and 3¾" Blocks

Use red lines on Mini Geese Ruler Two. Square to ¾" x 1½" Finished Size or 1¼" x 2" including seams.

6. Stack four red Geese on left, and four green Geese on right.

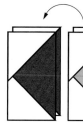

Make four red Geese.   *Make four green Geese.*

7. Flip right sides together. Sew into pairs.

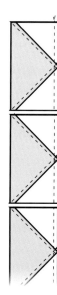

8. Press seams toward red.

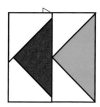

Making Blue/Yellow Geese

1. Place one blue square right sides together and centered on one Background square.

2. Repeat with one blue square centered on one yellow square.

12" Block	6" and 3¾" Blocks
5½" and 7"	3" and 4½"

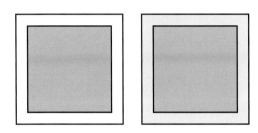

3. Draw diagonal line corner to corner on both sets of squares. Sew ¼" from both sides of drawn line. Cut on drawn line.

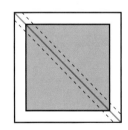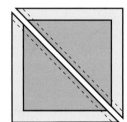

4. Press seams toward large triangle.

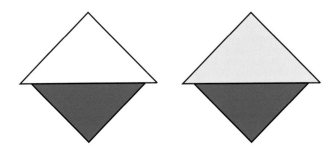

5. Place two sets of blue/Background right sides together with blue/yellow.

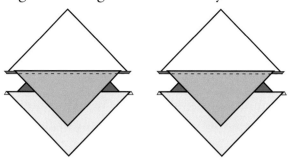

6. Draw a diagonal line. Sew ¼" from both sides of diagonal line. Cut on diagonal line. Clip seam and press open.

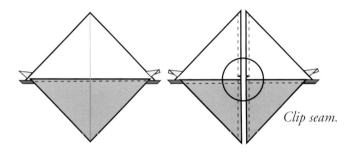

Clip seam.

7. Trim out four yellow/blue/Background Geese, and four mirror image yellow/blue/Background Geese.

12" Block

Use green lines on Mini Geese Ruler One. Square to 2" x 4" Finished Size or 2½" x 4½" including seams.

6" and 3¾" Blocks

Use red lines on Mini Geese Ruler Two. Square to ¾" x 1½" Finished Size or 1¼" x 2" including seams.

8. Make two mirror image stacks.

9. Set right stack aside for extra block.

12" Block	6" and 3¾" Blocks
2" x 4" finished size	¾" x 1½" finished size

Use this stack for block.   *Set this stack aside for extra block.*

Sewing Block Together

Use ¼" seam allowance.
Do not use a scant ¼" seam.

1. Lay out Geese with Center.

12" Block	6" and 3¾" Blocks
2½" square	1¼" square

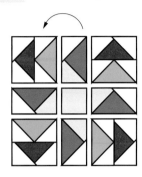

2. Flip middle vertical row right sides together to vertical row on left.

3. Assembly-line sew. Do not clip connecting threads.

4. Open. Flip right vertical row to middle vertical row.

5. Assembly-line sew. Do not clip apart.

6. Turn. Sew remaining rows, pressing seams away from yellow/blue.

7. Press just sewn seams away from center.

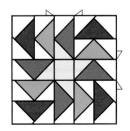

Adding Framing Border to 12" and 6" Blocks

Do not sew Framing Border to 3¾" block.

1. Sew strips to two opposite sides with block on top.

12" Block	6" Block
1¾" x 11"	1¾" x 5"

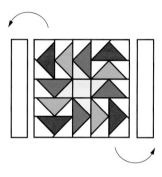

2. Set seams, open, and press toward Border. Trim even with block.

3. Repeat with remaining two sides.

12" Block	6" Block
1¾" x 13"	1¾" x 7"

4. Square block.

12" Block	6" Block
12½" square	6½" square

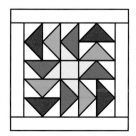

Block for 12" Finished Size Barn

1. Make 3¾" finished size Geese block following directions for 6" finished size block.

2. **Do not add Framing Border.**

3. Block should measure 4¼".

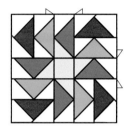

 ### Pinwheel Block for 6" Barn

Block is 1¼" finished size.

1. Cut one light and one dark 2" x 4" rectangle.

2. Place 2" x 4" rectangles right sides together. Draw a center line and diagonal lines.

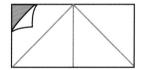

3. Sew ¼" from both sides of diagonal lines.

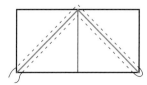

4. Cut on all lines.

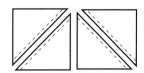

5. Square to 1¼" with 6½" Triangle Square Up Ruler.

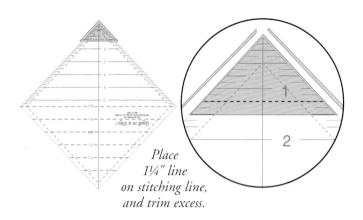

Place 1¼" line on stitching line, and trim excess.

6. Set seam with dark on top. Open. Press toward dark. Trim tips.

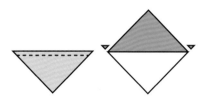

7. Lay out in Windmill design and sew together. Open center seam and "swirl". See "swirling" on page 46.

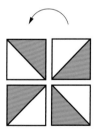

8. Patch should measure 2". Trim if necessary.

Gambrel Roof Barn

Eleanor built her silo out of brick, a rare material, as opposed to concrete, metal, or wood slats. A mama shares a milk break with her newborn calf, while a hungry pig looks on.

Teresa Varnes made her barn and silo out of the same non-directional fabric. Her rooster in the hayloft contemplates flight!

From about 1900 to 1940, many large dairy barns were built in Northern USA with gambrel, or hip roofs to maximize the size of the hayloft above the dairy roof. They have become associated with the popular image of a dairy farm. While manure handling and milking equipment made some advancements since early 1900's, many small dairy farms still milk their herds in barns configured nearly one hundred years ago.

Mid nineteenth century farmers borrowed the silo concept from the design of corn cellars constructed by Native Americans.

Amazingly, the small 3¾ " block has twelve geese patches, the smallest size Quilt in a Day makes!

Patty Knoechel planted sunflowers in her pasture, rich with manure! Directional clouds float by.

6" Barn has a 1½" Pinwheel Block.

Skill Level – Easy

Supplies
- Permanent marking pen
- Template Plastic

Permanent marking pen

	12" Finished Barn with 3¾" Geese Block	**6" Finished Barn** with 1½" Pinwheel Block
Directional Sky — First measurement is height. Second measurement is width.		
Non-directional Barn Roof	(2) 2½" x 5" or	(2) 1¾" x 3½" or
Or Directional Barn Roof	(2) 2½" x 5" and	(2) 1¾" x 3½" and
and Directional Barn Roof	(2) 5" x 2½"	(2) 3½" x 1¾"
Sides of Roof	(2) 2" squares	(2) 1¼" squares
Above Silo	(1) 3¼" x 3¾"	(1) 1½" x 2"
Yellow		
Hay Door	(1) 2½" square or (1) 2½" Fussy Cut	(1) 1½" square or (1) 1½" Fussy Cut
Directional Red — First measurement is height. Second measurement is width.		
Non-directional Barn Roof	(2) 2½" x 5" or	(2) 1¾" x 3½" or
Or Directional Barn Roof	(2) 2½" x 5" and	(2) 1¾" x 3½" and
and Directional Barn Roof	(2) 5" x 2½"	(2) 3½" x 1¾"
Bottom of Hay Door	(1) 1½" x 2½"	(1) 1" x 1½"
Sides of Hay Door	(2) 3½" x 2½"	(2) 2" x 1½"
Sides of Block	(2) 4¼" x 3"	(2) 2" squares
Bottom Row	(1) 2" x 9½"	(1) 1¼" x 5"
Silo	(1) 7½" x 3¾"	(1) 4" x 2"
Black		
Top of Silo	(1) 2½" x 4"	(1) 1¼" x 2"
Green		
Ground	(1) 3" x 13"	(1) 2" x 7"
Template Plastic	(1) 2" x 3½"	(1) 1¼" x 2"
Non-Woven Fusible Interfacing	(1) 2½" x 4"	(1) 1¼" x 2"

Making Barn Roof Pieces

1. Lay out pairs of rectangles **wrong sides together** in both Barn and Sky fabrics. Lay out one set of each for non-directional. Lay out two sets of each for directional. Illustrations show directional fabric.

12" Block	6" Block
2½" x 5"	1¾" x 3½"
5" x 2½"	3½" x 1¾"

Top Roof Row   *Hay Door Row*

2. Layer cut on one diagonal.

3. Stack Barn and Sky triangles right side up. Place two in each stack. The sets are mirror image of each other.

4. Flip right sides together.

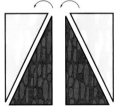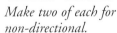  

Make two of each for non-directional.   *Make one set of each for directional. One triangle from each is extra.*

5. **Extend ⅜" tip at both ends.** Assembly-line sew.

6. Set seams with Barn on top, open, and press toward Barn.

Squaring Roof Pieces

1. Find Pattern Sheet in back of book.

2. Place rectangle from template plastic on pattern and trace diagonal line. Note diagonal line is ⅛" in from both corners.

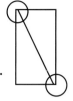

12" Block	6" Block
2" x 3½"	1¼" x 2"

3. Lay out left and right sides of each.

Top Roof Row   *Hay Door Row*

4. Place template on right piece. Trace around template.

5. Flip template over. Place template on left patch. Trace around template.

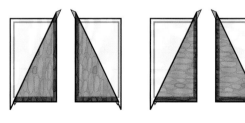

6. Cut on lines with ruler and rotary cutter.

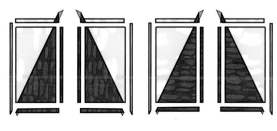

Sewing Top Roof Row Together

1. Lay out Roof with Sky Squares. For locking seam, **repress seam on right piece toward Sky.**

12" Block	6" Block
2" squares	1¼" squares

2. Flip Roof pieces right sides together. Lock together at seams, and sew. Press seam open.

   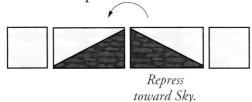

   Repress toward Sky.

3. Sew Sky squares to each side of Roof.

   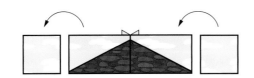

4. Press seams toward Sky squares.

5. Measure width.

   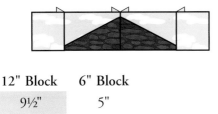

12" Block	6" Block
9½"	5"

 ## Sewing Hay Door Row Together

1. Sew Bottom of Hay Door to Hay Door. Press toward bottom of Hay Door.

12" Block	6" Block
1½" x 2½"	1" x 1½"
2½" square	1½" square

   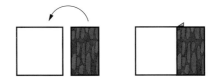

2. Sew Sides of Hay Door and Roof pieces with Hay Door.

12" Block	6" Block
3½" x 2½"	2" x 1½"

   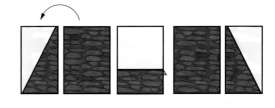

3. Press toward Barn rectangles.

4. Measure width.

12" Block	6" Block
9½"	5"

Sewing Quilt Row Together

1. Lay out quilt block with two Barn rectangles. Substitute Pinwheel for 6" Block.

12" Block	6" Block
4¼" x 3"	2" squares

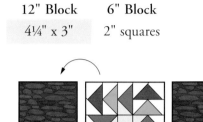

2. Sew seams with Barn on top, open, and press toward Barn.

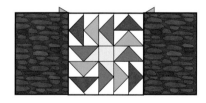

3. Measure width. Trim if necessary.

12" Block	6" Block
9½"	5"

Sewing Barn Together

1. Flip Roof row right sides together to Hay Door row. Lock seams and sew.

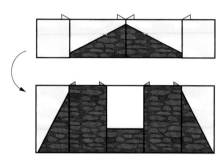

2. Press seam toward top row.

3. Add Quilt Block row. Sew with block on top. Press seam toward top.

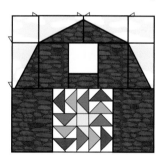

4. Sew Barn strip to bottom. Press seams toward strip.

12" Block	6" Block
2" x 9½"	1¼" x 5"

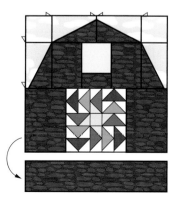

Sewing Silo

1. Place non-woven fusible interfacing smooth side up.

2. Place interfacing on top of Silo pattern and trace with permanent marking pen.

12" Block	6" Block
2½" x 4"	1¼" x 2"

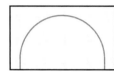

3. Place fusible side of interfacing against right side of Top of Silo fabric.

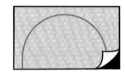

4. Lighten pressure on presser foot, and sew on line with 20 stitches per inch.

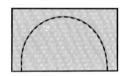

5. Trim ⅛" from seam, and turn right side out.

6. Place on Sky piece ¼" **from left edge.** Fuse in place.

12" Block	6" Block
3¼" x 3¾"	1½" x 2"

7. Stitch around outside edge with straight stitch or zig-zag stitch.

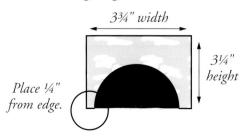

3¾" width

3¼" height

Place ¼" from edge.

8. Sew Top of Silo to Silo.

12" Block	6" Block
7½" x 3¾"	4" x 2"

9. Press seam toward Silo.

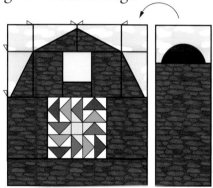

10. Sew Silo to Barn. Press seam toward Silo.

11. Straighten bottom edge.

12. Optional: Satin stitch on roof line with black thread.

Finishing Block

1. Sew Ground to block.

12" Block	6" Block
3" x 13"	2" x 7"

2. Trim on bottom and right edges.

12" Block	6" Block
12½" square	6½" square

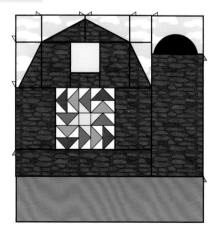

Country Clothesline

Supplies
Point Turner
Ball Point Bodkin
Fat Drinking Straw

Wallhanging features 6" Gambrel Roof Barn. Cut pieces for 6" Barn following directions beginning on page 112.

Substitute 2" x 7" Ground with 6" x 11½" Ground, and 2" quilt from quilt fabric.

Patricia Knoechel
Amie Potter
11½" x 12½"

Cut these additional pieces.

Sky
Top	(1) 3" x 11½"
Left Side	(1) 5" x 2½"
Right Side	(1) 5" x 3½"

Floral Landscape
Left Side	(1) 2¾" x 2½"
Right Side	(1) 3¾" x 3½"

Non-woven Fusible Interfacing
Left Side	(1) 2½" x 2¾"
Right Side	(1) 3½" x 3¾"

Green
Ground	(1) 6" x 11½"

Miniature Quilts from Quilt Fabric
Barn Quilt	(1) 2" square
Clothesline Quilts	(3) 3" squares

Backings for Miniature Quilts
Clothesline Quilts	(3) 3" squares
Backing and Batting	(1) 15" square of each
Binding	¼ yd (2) 2½" strips
Cord for Clothesline	(1) 12" piece *(Handle from gift bag works great)*

Making Barn

1. Sew 6" Barn following directions beginning on page 112.

2. Place fusible side of non-woven fusible interfacing against right side of Floral Landscape fabric. Draw a curved Skyline across top edge.

Left Side	Right Side
2¾" x 2½"	3¾" x 3½"

3. Sew on line, and trim to ⅛". Turn right side out.

4. Fuse to left and right Sky pieces, lining up outside edges.

Left Side	Right Side
5" x 2½"	5" x 3½"

5. Sew Side and Top Sky pieces to Barn. Press seams toward Sky.

Download printable quilt blocks on www.quiltinaday.com/eleanorandcompany/freepattern/

Making Quilts

1. Turn top edges of Clothesline quilts and matching backings under ½" and press. Place right sides together.

2. Sew around outside edges with ¼" seam, starting and stopping ½" from top edges. Trim. Turn right side out.

3. Place cord through top edges of three Clothesline quilts.

4. Hand slip stitch top edges together.

5. Layer Wallhanging with batting and backing and quilt.

6. Pin cord to sides 5" from bottom edge.

7. Bind, enclosing ends of cord in binding.

Peaceful Pasture

Supplies
Point Turner
Ball Point Bodkin
Fat Drinking Straw

Ball Point Bodkin

Cut and sew pieces for 3¾"
Flying Geese block and 12"
Gambrel Roof Barn block
beginning on page 112.
Substitute 3" x 13" Grass with
6" x 20" Grass.

Patricia Knoechel
Amie Potter
22" x 24"

Cut additional pieces listed below.

Directional Sky	⅓ yd
Cut height by width	
Sky Inside Rickrack	
Sides	(2) 10½" x 4"
Top of Barn	(1) 2½" x 20"
Sky Outside Rickrack	
Sides	(2) 17½" x 2¾"
Top	(1) 2¾" x 24"

Grass	⅜ yd
Grass Inside Rickrack	
Under Barn	(1) 6" x 20"
Grass Outside Rickrack	
Right Side	(1) 12" x 2¾"
Left Side	(1) 10" x 2¾"
Bottom	(1) 4" x 24"

Small Scale Floral Fabric	
Inside Rickrack	(2) 6" x 4"

Large Scale Floral Fabric	
	(1) 7" Fussy Cut

Barnyard Animals	Fat Quarter
	2" to 4" tall
Backing	¾ yd
Batting	28" x 30"
Binding	¼ yd
	(3) 2½" strips
Jumbo Rickrack	(1) 2½ yd package
Non-woven Fusible Interfacing	¼ yd
	(2) 4" x 6"
	(2) 2¾" x 4"

Sewing Grass and Sky to Barn

1. Place two 6" x 4" Floral fabrics right side up with fusible interfacing on top, smooth side up. Pin.

2. Repeat with 12" x 2¾" and 10" x 2¾" pieces of Grass with 2¾" x 4" pieces of fusible interfacing.

3. With permanent marking pen, draw "horizon" line on each piece. Follow the print in the fabric, or create your own "horizon".

4. Stitch on lines with 18 stitches per inch. Trim ⅛" away and turn. Smooth out curves with point turner.

5. Place Floral fabric on 10½" x 4" Sky fabric. Fuse in place. Sew edge by hand or machine. Repeat with Grass and Sky.

6. Place Sides and sew to Barn. Press seams toward Sky.

7. Sew 2½" x 20" Sky to top of Barn. Press seam toward Sky. Trim ends even.

8. Sew 6" x 20" Grass to bottom of Barn. Press seam toward Grass.

Sewing Rickrack around Barnyard

1. Set machine for long stitch length and scant ¼" seam.

2. On sides, place points of rickrack along raw edge. Sew with rickrack next to feed dogs to avoid gathering.

3. Repeat sewing rickrack to top and bottom.

Finishing Barn

1. Sew Grass/Sky to Sides.

2. Sew 4" x 24" Grass to bottom, and 2¾" x 24" Sky to top.

3. Applique barnyard animals.

4. Quilt and bind.

Americana Star Block

The Americana Star block, proudly displayed on a weathered gambrel roof barn, is a symbol of patriotism. A celebration of country pride goes hand in hand with a good old fashioned county fair on the Fourth of July.

Early in the 1900s, boys and girls were encouraged to exhibit animal entries through a new national youth movement called 4-H. Their 4-leaf clover insignia places emphasis on Head, Heart, Hands, and Health.

Today, the county fair is one of the year's main events for families that spans generations. Competition is friendly! The kitchen is crowded in the days before the fair, as the deadline for baked goods such as breads, cakes, pies, jellies, jams, canned vegetables and candies draws near. Those handy with a needle and thread compete in the textile competition. Hobby and craft divisions provide many with an opportunity to display their pastimes.

photo –Brian Steuel

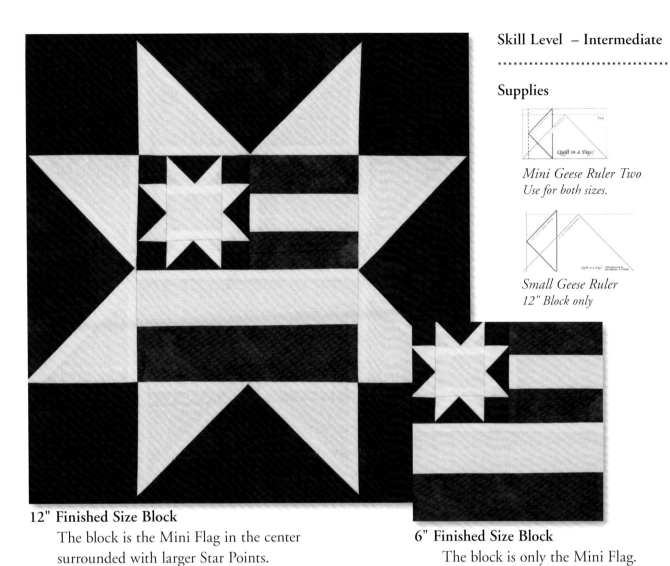

Supplies

Mini Geese Ruler Two
Use for both sizes.

Small Geese Ruler
12" Block only

12" Finished Size Block

The block is the Mini Flag in the center surrounded with larger Star Points.

6" Finished Size Block

The block is only the Mini Flag.

	12" Finished Block	**6" Finished Block**
Background		
Large Star Points	(1) 9" square	____
Mini Star Points	(1) 4½" square	(1) 4½" square
Mini Star Center	(1) 2" square	(1) 2" square
Wide Stripe	(1) 2" x 6½"	(1) 2" x 6½"
Narrow Stripe	(1) 1½" x 3½"	(1) 1½" x 3½"
Red		
Wide Stripe	(1) 2" x 6½"	(1) 2" x 6½"
Narrow Stripes	(2) 1½" x 3½"	(2) 1½" x 3½"
Blue		
Large Star Points	(1) 7½" square	____
Large Star Corners	(4) 3½" squares	____
Mini Star Points	(1) 3" square	(1) 3" square
Mini Star Corners	(4) 1¼" squares	(4) 1¼" squares

123

Making Star Points

Star Points are made the same as Geese patches.

1. Place Background squares right side up. Place both sizes for 12" block. Place only smaller size for 6" block.

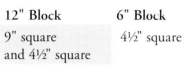

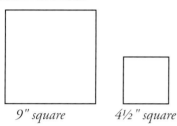

9" square   *4½" square*

2. Place Blue squares right sides together and centered on Background Star Points squares.

12" Block	6" Block
7½" square and 3" square	3" square

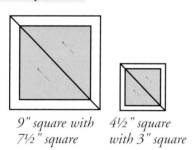

9" square with 7½" square   *4½" square with 3" square*

3. Draw diagonal line across squares. Pin.

4. Sew ¼" from both sides of drawn line. Cut on drawn line. Keep two sizes separated.

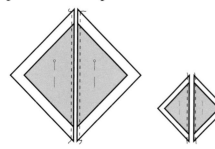

5. Follow Geese directions beginning on page 26.

Squaring Up Large Star Points for 12" Block Only

1. Use Small Geese Ruler for 3" x 6" Finished Size Star Points.

2. Cut InvisiGRIP™ ½" smaller than Geese ruler and place on underside of ruler.

3. Place patch on small cutting mat.

4. Line up ruler's **green lines** on 45° sewn lines. Line up dotted line with peak of triangle for ¼" seam allowance.

5. Cut block in half to separate two patches.

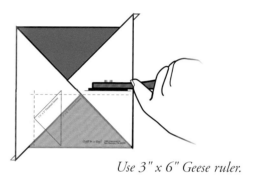

Use 3" x 6" Geese ruler.

6. While turning mat, trim off excess fabric. Hold ruler securely on fabric so it does not shift while cutting.

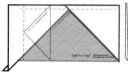

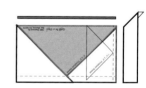

7. Check for ¼" seam allowance on top edge. Seams go into corners on bottom edge.

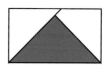

Patches should measure 3½" x 6½" including seam allowance.

Squaring Up Small Star Points for 6" and 12" Blocks

1. Use Mini Geese Ruler Two. Place InvisiGRIP™ on bottom side of ruler.

2. Place patch on small cutting mat right side up. Place Mini Ruler in vertical position on patch. **Line up ruler's red solid lines on sewn lines for ¾" x 1½" Finished Geese.** Line up red dotted line with peak of triangle for ¼" seam.

3. Hold ruler securely on fabric so it doesn't shift while cutting.

4. Cut block in half, and separate two patches.

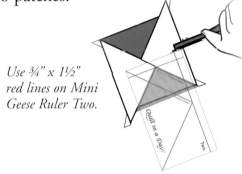

Use ¾" x 1½" red lines on Mini Geese Ruler Two.

5. Trim off excess fabric on right.

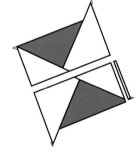

6. Turn patch. Do not turn ruler. Trim off excess fabric on right and top. **Patch should measure 1¼" x 2".**

7. Repeat with remaining half.

Patches should measure 1¼" x 2" including seam allowance.

Sewing 6" Mini Flag Together

Star is 3" finished size. Star with stripes is 6" finished size. Sew for both 12" and 6" finished blocks.

1. Lay out Mini Star with 1¼" x 2" Star Points, one 2" square Background for Center, and four 1¼" blue squares for Corners.

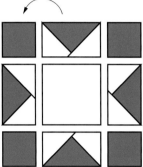

2. Flip middle vertical row to left, right sides together. Assembly-line sew vertical seams. Do not clip connecting threads.

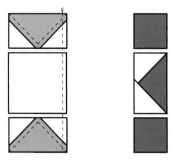

3. Open and add right vertical row.

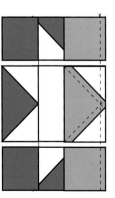

4. Turn. Sew right row, pressing top seams away from Star Points, and lunderneath seams toward Star Center. Seams lock together.

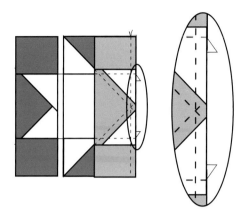

Sewing Stripes Together

1. Lay out two red and one Background 1½" x 3½" strips.

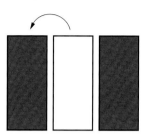

2. Lay out one Background and one red 2" x 6½" strip.

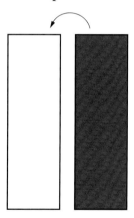

5. Sew second horizontal row, repeating seams. Set seams, open, and press.

6. Check from wrong side. Horizontal seams should be pressed away from center.

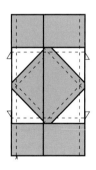 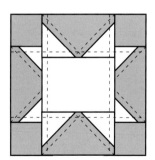

7. Check from right side for ¼" seams.

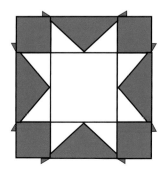

3. Assembly-line sew together.

4. Press seams toward red.

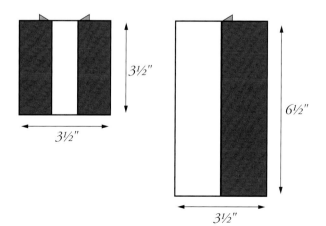

Sewing 6" Flag Block Together

1. Sew Narrow Stripes to Mini Star.

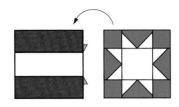

2. Press seams toward Stripe.

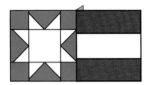

3. Sew Wide Stripes to Mini Star.

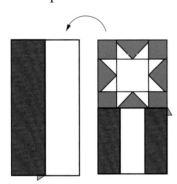

4. Press seam toward Background.

5. Measure. **Block should measure 6½" square. Sliver trim from Stripes if necessary.**

6. The 6" Finished Size Block is now completed.

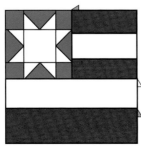

Block should measure 6½" square, including seam allowance.

Sewing 12" Large Star Together

1. Place 3½" x 6½" Star Points and four blue 3½" Corners with Mini Flag.

2. Flip middle vertical row right sides together to left vertical row.

3. Assembly-line sew.

4. Open. Flip right vertical row to middle vertical row, and assembly-line sew.

5. Turn. Sew remaining rows, pressing seams away from Large Star Points, and toward Flag block. Seams lock together.

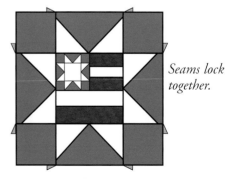

Seams lock together.

6. Press just sewn seams away from center.

Americana Star Wallhanging

For this patriotic project, make three 12" Americana Star blocks. Yardage chart on right includes three Americana Star blocks plus setting fabrics.

Eleanor Burns
Amie Potter
24" x 52"

Background	Three 12" Finished Blocks Plus Setting Fabric
Background	**⅔ yd**
Lattice	(4) 2½" strips cut into
	(10) 2½" x 12½"
	(1) 9" strip cut into
Large Star Points	(3) 9" squares
Mini Star Points	(3) 4½" squares
	(1) 2" strip cut into
Mini Star Center	(3) 2" squares
Wide Stripe	(1) 2" x 21"
Narrow Stripe	(1) 1½" x 12"
Red Stripe	**1½ yds**
Border	(3) 4½" strips cut lengthwise
	(1) 2" strip cut lengthwise into
Wide Stripe	(1) 2" x 21"
Narrow Stripes	(2) 1½" x 12"
Backing	Remainder
Blue	**½ yd**
	(1) 7½" strip cut into
Large Star Points	(3) 7½" squares
Mini Star Points	(3) 3" squares
Mini Star Corners	(12) 1¼" squares
	(2) 3½" strips cut into
Large Star Corners	(12) 3½" squares
Yellow	**⅛ yd**
	(1) 2½" strip cut into
Corner Stones	(8) 2½" squares
Binding	**½ yd**
	(4) 3" strips
Batting	**30" x 58"**

Sewing Top Together

1. Make three 12" Americana Star blocks.

2. Lay out three Star blocks with Lattice and Cornerstones.

3. Assembly-line sew vertical rows together.

4. Sew remaining rows, pressing seams toward Lattice.

5. Press just sewn seams away from Stars.

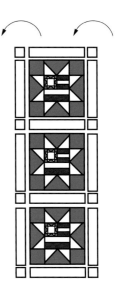

Adding Borders

1. Measure, pin, and sew side Borders.

2. Set seams with Border on top, open, and press toward Border.

3. Measure, pin, and sew top and bottom Borders.

4. Set seams with Border on top, open, and press toward Border.

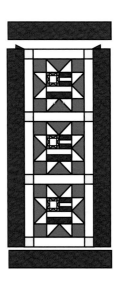

5. Layer with batting and backing.

6. Quilt.

7. *Optional:* To prepare a casing sewn on by machine, "stitch in the ditch" in top Border seam from right side.

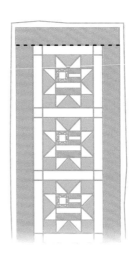

Sewing Casing and Binding

1. Cut a casing 5½" x 22" from any left-over fabric.

2. Turn under two narrow ends, and edge stitch.

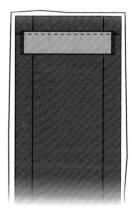

3. Place casing right sides together to backing, lining up top edge of casing ½" above "stitch in the ditch" line from top Border seam. Pin in place.

4. "Stitch in the ditch" again along Border seam from right side to catch top edge of casing.

5. Fold casing up, and pin in place.

6. Bind quilt, enclosing casing in Binding.

Stars Galore (Quilt on Right)

Sally Murray shared these measurements for a second Star block and Lattice:

The Star is 6" finished size using 1½" x 3" **Small Flying Geese Ruler**, plus stripes. Follow illustrations on pages 125 - 127 to make a 12" finished size block.

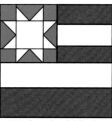

12" finished block

Background

(1) 6" square for Star Points
(1) 3½" square for Star Center
(1) 2½" x 6½" Stripe
(1) 3½" x 12½" Stripe
(1) 3" x 12½" per Lattice

Blue

(1) 4½" square for Star Points
(4) 2" square for Star Corners
(4) 1¾" squares Lattice Star Points per Lattice
(1) 3" square Lattice Star Center per Lattice

Red

(2) 2½" x 6½" Stripe
(1) 3½" x 12½" Stripe

Ribbon Border

Follow directions in *Victory Quilts* by Eleanor Burns beginning on page 222.

One Lattice

Draw diagonal lines on wrong side of 1¾" squares. Place one on opposite corners of Lattice, right sides together. Sew on diagonal lines.

Trim ¼" from seams, and press open.

Place remaining two 1¾" squares and stitch on lines.

Trim, and press open.

Stars Galore

Sally loves her quilt, and believes it is the prettiest patriotic quilt she has ever seen. She may be right! A lover of country, Sally started making 12" Americana Star blocks and created a second flag waving 12" block to add to her red, white, and blue quilt. See measurements on the left for making one 12" Star Block.

Sally Murray
84" x 84"

Bank Barn with Flying Kite Block

In the early morning, the rooster begins crowing, heralding the beginning of a brand new day. The farm awakes. Chores are started with the animals as life on the farm begins. Eggs are gathered, goats milked, and livestock are fed and turned out to pasture.

With scheduled chores, there wasn't much time for playing. One entertaining sport farm children enjoyed during days with good winds was flying kites.

Kansas City Star named this block Flying Kite in 1937, just before kite flying experienced resurgence with the military in the 1940's. In Grandmother Clark's 1931 book, the pattern was referred to as Pinwheel.

Skill Level – Easy

....

Supplies

6" x 12" Ruler

9½" Square Up Ruler

6" Square Up Ruler for
   3" and 1¾" Blocks

6½" Fussy Cut Ruler for 12" Block

3½" Fussy Cut Ruler for 6" Block

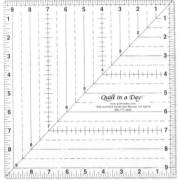

9½ " Square Up Ruler

*3½ " Fussy Cut
Ruler for 6" Block*

*6½ " Fussy Cut Ruler
for 12" Block*

	12" Finished Block For Large Barn Quilt	6" Finished Block For Small Barn Quilt	3" Finished Block For 12" Finished Barn	1¾" Finished Block For 6" Finished Barn
Background				
	(1) 7½" square (2) 2⅛" x 16"	(1) 4½" square (2) 1½" x 9"	(1) 2⅞" square (2) 1" x 5½"	(1) 2¼" square (2) ¾" x 5"
Medium Yellow				
	(1) 7½" square	(1) 4½" square	(1) 2⅞" square	(1) 2¼" square
Dark Blue				
	(1) 5¾" x 16"	(1) 3½" x 9"	(1) 2¼" x 5½"	(1) 1⅞" x 5"

133

Making Four Points

1. Draw an X on wrong side of Background square.

12" Block	6" Block	3" Block	1¾" Block
7½"	4½"	2⅞"	2¼"

5. Pivot again and stitch ¼" from diagonal line.

6. Repeat on second diagonal line.

2. Place Background square right sides together to same size Medium square. **Background must be on top.** Pin.

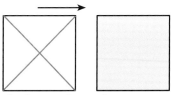

Background must be on top.

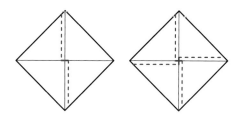

7. Press square.

8. Cut square apart on both **drawn** diagonal lines into four triangles.

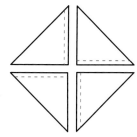

3. Turn. Sew ¼" from left side of diagonal line and stop at crossing diagonal line.

4. Leave needle in fabric, pivot, and sew on pencil line stopping ¼" past first diagonal line.

9. Stack triangles with Medium on top.

10. Open and press seams to Medium.

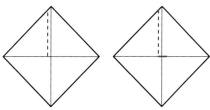

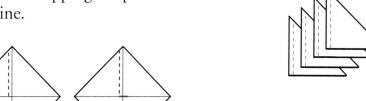

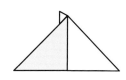

Making Four

1. Lay out two Background with Dark in center.

12" Block	6" Block	3" Block	1¾" Block
2⅛" x 16"	1½" x 9"	1" x 5½"	¾" x 5"
5¾" x 16"	3½" x 9"	2¼" x 5½"	1⅞" x 5"

2. Sew three strips together.

3. Set seams with Dark on top. Open, and press toward Dark.

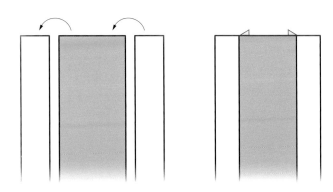

4. Measure from top of first Background to top of Second Background.

12" Block	6" Block	3" Block	1¾" Block
7" – 7⅛"	4" – 4⅛"	2⅜" – 2½"	1¾" – 1⅞"

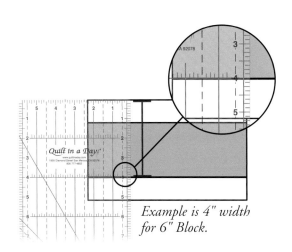

Example is 4" width for 6" Block.

5. Trim left edge. Cut into two pieces that same measurement.

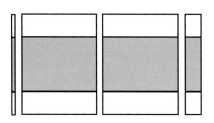

12" Block	6" Block	3" Block	1¾" Block
7" – 7⅛"	4" – 4⅛"	2⅜" – 2½"	1¾" – 1⅞"

6. Place ruler on Background at top left corner and on Dark at bottom right.

7. Carefully cut on angle. The first patch is complete. Set aside.

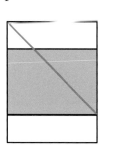 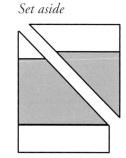

Set aside

8. Place ruler on Dark at top left and on Background at bottom right. Carefully cut on angle.

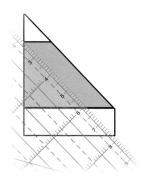

9. Discard middle section.

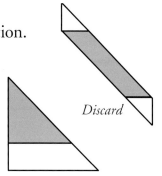

Discard

Save

135

Sewing Four

1. Stack four of each.

2. Flip piece on right to piece on left, right sides together. Assembly-line sew.

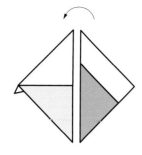

3. Set seam with Dark/Background on top, open and press toward Dark/Background.

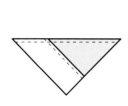 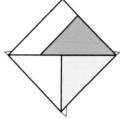

4. Square patches.

12" Block	6" Block	3" Block	1¾" Block
6½" Fussy Cut Ruler	3½" Fussy Cut Ruler	2" Square	1⅜" Square

12" and 6" Blocks:

Use appropriate Fussy Cut Ruler. Line up X on Fussy Cut Ruler with diagonal seams, and trim.

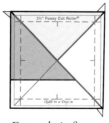

Example is for 6" Block

3" Block:

Place 1" in upper right corner. Place diagonal line on diagonal seam with dark and medium in upper right corner. Place 2" measurement on medium. Trim right and top sides.

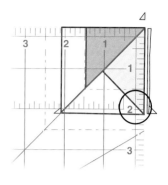

Turn patch. Do not turn ruler. Place 2" measurement on outside edges, and trim right and top sides.

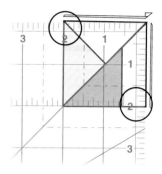

1¾" Block:

Place 1" in upper right corner. Place diagonal line on diagonal seam with dark and medium in upper right corner. Place 1⅜" measurement on medium. Trim right and top sides.

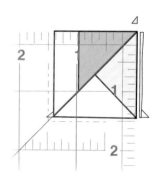

Turn patch. Do not turn ruler. Place 1⅜" measurement on outside edges, and trim right and top sides.

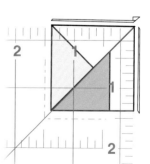

Sewing Block Together

1. Lay out patches.

2. Flip right vertical row right sides together to left vertical row. Lock seams.

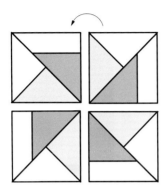

3. Assembly-line sew. Do not clip connecting thread.

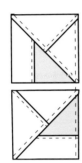

4. Turn. Flip vertical row on right to vertical row on left.

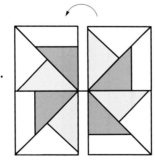

5. Lock seams, pushing top seam up, and underneath seam down. Sew.

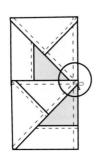

6. Clip connecting thread in center and remove three straight stitches in vertical seam on both sides. See red thread.

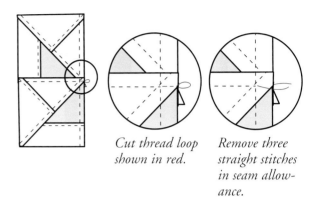

Cut thread loop shown in red.   *Remove three straight stitches in seam allowance.*

7. Place on pressing mat wrong side up. Push top vertical seam to right, and bottom vertical seam to left. Center will pop open and make a little pinwheel.

8. Press center flat with your finger. Press so seams swirl around center.

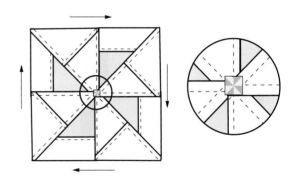

9. Square up block.

12" Block	6" Block	3" Block	1¾" Block
12½"	6½"	3½"	2¼"

Flying Kite Quilt

Teresa Varnes designed and sewed this quaint Flying Kite quilt with the charm of a Depression era quilt.

Make thirty-five 6½" Blocks.

Five Dark Fat Quarters	
	(4) 3½" strips cut into
	(7) 3½" x 9" rectangles from each

Five Medium Fat Quarters	
	(2) 4½" x 20" strips cut into
	(7) 4½" squares from each

Background	2½ yds
Blocks	(5) 4½" strips cut into
	(35) 4½" squares
	(20) 1½" strips cut into
	(70) 1½" x 9" rectangles
Lattice	(14) 2" strips cut into
	(82) 2" x size of Block

Pink	¼ yd
Cornerstones	(3) 2" strips cut into
	(48) 2" squares

Yellow	⅓ yd
First Border	(5) 2" strips

Blue	1¼ yds
Second Border	(6) 6½" strips

Straight Binding	⅝ yd
	(6) 3" strips
or **Optional** **Bias Binding**	1 yd
	2¼" bias strips sewn into 7 yd length
Backing	3½ yds
Batting	62" x 78"

Skill Level – Easy

Supplies
6" x 12" Ruler
3½" Fussy Cut Ruler
Scallops, Vines & Waves Template

Scallops, Vines & Waves Template

Making Flying Kite Quilt

1. Pair 3½" x 9" rectangles from one dark fat quarter with 4½" squares from one medium fat quarter. Make seven 6" finished size blocks from each set, making a total of thirty-five.

2. Lay out blocks in five across and seven rows down.

3. Place 2" x 6½" Lattice and 2" Cornerstones between blocks.

4. Assembly-line sew vertical rows together. Do not clip connecting threads.

5. Sew remaining rows, pressing seams toward Lattice for locking seams.

6. From wrong side, press seams toward Lattice.

7. Sew 2" First Border and 6½" Second Border to quilt. Press seams toward Borders.

8. **Optional:** Mark wave on outside edge with Scallops, Vines, and Wave Template. Mark seven waves 8"- 8¼" long on sides and five waves 8" – 8¼" long on top and bottom. Follow instructions included in ruler package.

9. Quilt and bind.

Teresa Varnes
Amie Potter
54" x 70"

Bank Barn

Often referred to as a Pennsylvania bank barn, they were built into a slope, or "bank", allowing entry to the upper floor from the uphill side, and lower floor from the downhill side. Usually the lower level held livestock stalls and the upper level was a threshing floor, thus the grain and animals were separated for sanitary reasons.

In these two blocks, Patricia Knoechel shows how to cleverly change the look of the bank barn. In the first barn, Patty "painted" a beautiful purple and yellow Flying Kite block. She coordinated the landscape with rippling rows of purple flowers. Fabrics representing grass and rock foundation make the block look more realistic.

In the second photo, Patty remodeled the barn into a cute livable cottage by adding a charming paned window with lace curtains and window box overflowing with flowers. Quiet bunnies check out her stone walkway. Notice the rolling hills in the distance.

Skill Level – Easy

••

Supplies
  6" Square Up Ruler

6" Square Up Ruler

	12" Finished Barn	6" Finished Barn
Directional Red	First measurement is height. Second measurement is width	
Roof	(2) 4½" x 5½"	(2) 2¾" x 3½"
Sides of Block	(2) 4" x 3¼"	(2) 2¼" x 2"
Bottom of Barn	(1) 2½" x 9½"	(1) 1½" x 5¼"
Directional Sky	First measurement is height. Second measurement is width	
Roof	(2) 4½" x 5½"	(2) 2¾" x 3½"
Left Side	(1) 9½" x 2¼"	(1) 5" x 1½"
Right Side	(1) 13" x 2¼"	(1) 7" x 1½"
Ground	First measurement is height. Second measurement is width	
	(1) 4½" x 10½"	(1) 2½" x 6"
	(1) 3¾" x 2¼"	(1) 2" x 1½"
Brick		
	(1) 4½" x 10½"	(1) 2½" x 6"
Framing Border		
	(2) ¾" x 3¾"	
	(2) ¾" x 4¼"	
Fussy Cut Animals		

Making Flying Kite Block

12" Barn

1. Make 3" finished size Flying Kite block.

2. Sew ¾" x 3¾" Framing Border to two sides. Press seams toward Framing Border. Square ends with block.

3. Sew ¾" x 4¼" Framing Border to remaining two sides. Press seams toward Framing Border. Square block to 4".

6" Barn

1. Make 1¾" finished size Flying Kite block.

2. **Do not add Framing Border.**

3. Square block to 2¼".

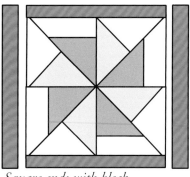

Square ends with block.

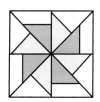

 ## Making Roof

1. Stack pairs of Sky rectangles and Roof rectangles **wrong sides together.**

12" Barn	6" Barn
4½" x 5½"	2¾" x 3½"

2. Layer cut from corner to corner.

3. Lay out pairs right side up. Discard remaining parts of rectangles.

4. Flip blue right sides together to red, and assembly-line sew.

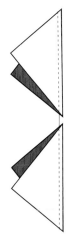

5. Set seam on left patch with blue on top, open, and press toward blue.

6. Set seam on right patch with red on top, open, and press toward red.

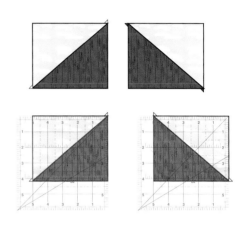

7. Square patches with 6" Square Up Ruler.

12" Barn	6" Barn
4" x 5"	2¼" x 2¾"

8. Sew together, locking seams.

9. Press center seam open.

 Adding Sides to Quilt block

1. Sew Barn rectangles to each side of block, with block on top.

12" Barn	6" Barn
4" x 3¼"	2¼" x 2"

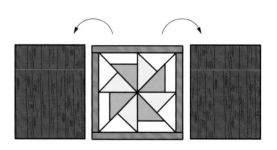

2. Press seams away from block.

3. Lay out with Roof, match center seam, and sew. *Sides are longer than Roof.*

4. Press seam toward Roof.

5. Place Bottom Row with Barn, and sew together. Press seam toward bottom.

6. Square patch. Trim from sides only.

12" Block	6" Block
9½" square	5" square

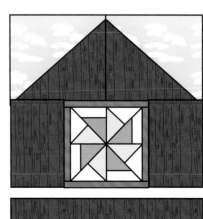

Sewing Ground and Brick

1. Place one Ground and one Brick rectangle right sides up.

12" Barn	6" Barn
4½" x 10½"	2½" x 6"

2. Cut from corner to corner.

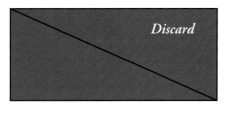
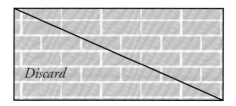

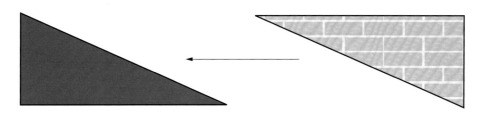

3. Lay out one patch. Discard other parts of rectangles.

4. Flip right sides together, let tips hang over on both ends, and sew.

5. Set seam with Ground on top, open, and press toward Ground.

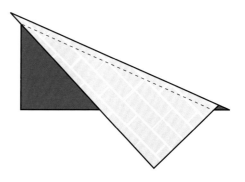

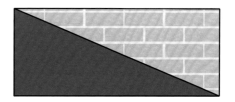

6. Square up patch with top left seam into corner. Botom right seam does not go into corner.

12" Block	6" Block
3¾" x 9½"	2" x 5"

7. Sew Ground/Brick to bottom of Barn. Press toward Barn.

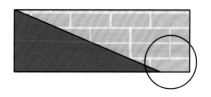

Finishing Barn

1. Place one Ground and one Brick rectangle right sides together.

2. Sew Ground to left Sky.

12" Barn	6" Barn
3¾" x 2¼"	2" x 1½"
9½" x 2¼"	5" x 1½"

3. Press seam toward Ground.

4. Sew left Sky to Barn, locking Ground seams with Barn. Press seam toward Sky.

5. Sew right Sky to Barn, and press toward Sky.

6. Square block from Sides and Bottom. Do not trim from top.

12" Barn	6" Barn
12½" square	6½" square

7. Applique animals to bank.

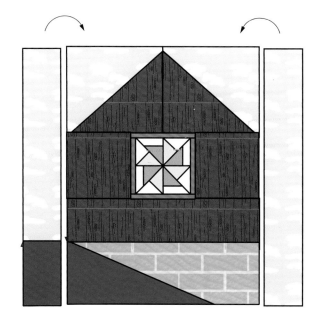

Dora's Delight Block

The Smidt barn sits on a well traveled road near Ulmer, Iowa. It features a gambrel roof with wood shingles, lightening rods, Dutch doors, and the original boards and batten. The barn quilt on the Smidt barn features the pattern Dora's Delight, which was published in the Farm Journal. Jeffrey Gutcheon appropriately called the block Road to Paradise. Mary and Coonie Scheidemantle, great grandparents of Eleanor Burns, owned a farm outside of Zelienople, PA. Their daughter, Dora Scheidemantle Druschel, was raised on the farm. Eleanor dedicates this block, Dora's Delight, to her maternal grandmother.

Mary and Coonie Scheidemantle

Dora Scheidemantle Druschel

photo – Brian Steutel

Skill Level – Easy

Supplies
- 6½" Triangle Square Up Ruler
- 4½" Fussy Cut Ruler
- 2½" Fussy Cut Ruler
- Triangle in a Square Ruler Set
- Small Cutting Mat

6½" Triangle Square Up Ruler
Use for both sizes.

4½" Fussy Cut Ruler
2½" Fussy Cut Ruler

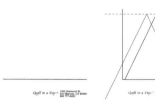

Triangle in a Square Ruler Set
Use for both sizes.

	12" Finished Block	6" Finished Block
Background		
Star Points	(1) 5" x 15"	(1) 3" x 10"
Corners	(1) 5" x 10"	(1) 3" x 6"
Dark Green		
Center Square	(1) 3¼" square	(1) 1⅞" square
Medium Green		
Corners	(1) 5" x 10"	(1) 3" x 6"
Yellow		
Center Triangles	(2) 3½" squares	(2) 2¼" squares
Red		
Star Points	(4) 3" x 6"	(4) 1⅞" x 3⅝"

Making Center Square

1. Cut two squares for Center Triangles in half on one diagonal. Stack.

12" Block	6" Block
3½" squares	2¼" squares

2. Center one triangle on each side of Center Square.

12" Block	6" Block
3¼" square	1⅞" square

3. Flip Center right sides together to triangle.

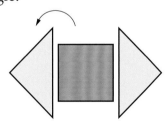

4. Sew with triangle on bottom so bias does not stretch.

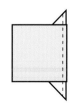 

5. Open. Repeat with second triangle.

6. Press seams toward triangles. Trim tips.

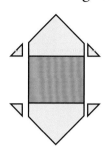

7. Sew triangles to two remaining sides.

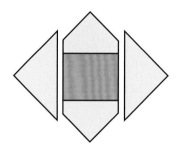

8. Press seams toward triangles.

9. Square with Fussy Cut Ruler.

12" Block	6" Block
4½" square	2½" square

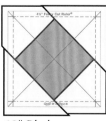

6" Block

12" Block

Place patch on small cutting mat. Center ruler on patch, with ¼" seam lines on ruler touching points on patch.

Trim four sides while turning mat.

Making Corners

1. Place Background rectangle right sides together to medium green rectangle.

12" Block	6" Block
5" x 10"	3" x 6"

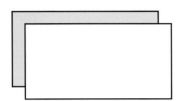

2. Draw center line.

3. Draw diagonal lines. Pin.

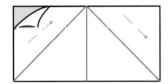

4. Sew ¼" seam on both sides of diagonal lines. Remove pins. Press.

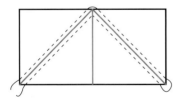

5. Cut apart on marked lines.

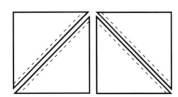

6. Square with 6½" Triangle Square Up Ruler.

12" Block	6" Block
4½" square	2½" square

12" Block
Place ruler's 4½" red dashed line on stitching line. Center ruler on patch. Trim two sides.

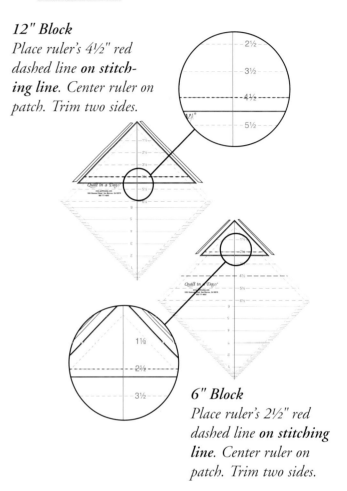

6" Block
Place ruler's 2½" red dashed line on stitching line. Center ruler on patch. Trim two sides.

7. Set seam with medium green on top.

8. Open, and press seam toward medium.

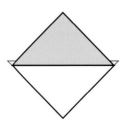

9. Trim tips.

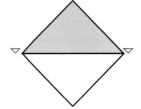

Cutting Star Points

1. Layer Star Point rectangles in pairs **wrong sides together.**

12" Block	3" Block
3" x 6"	1⅞" x 3⅝"

2. Layer cut pairs on one diagonal.

3. Sort Star Points right side up.

Cutting Background Triangles

1. Lay out Background strip right side up. Accurately line up top of Triangle Ruler with top of strip.

12" Block	6" Block
5" x 15"	3" x 10"

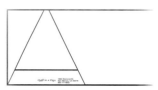 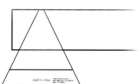

12" Block:
Line up top and bottom edges of Triangle Ruler with 5" strip.

6" Block:
Line up top edge of Triangle Ruler with strip. Keep ruler straight by lining up red line on mat's line.

2. Cut four triangles. Alternate direction of Triangle Ruler as you cut.

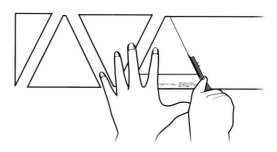

Sewing Star Points

1. Stack Background triangles right side up with Star Points.

2. Set right stack of Star Points aside.

3. Flip Background triangle right sides together to left Star Point. Star Point extends beyond Background to create a tip at flat top of triangle.

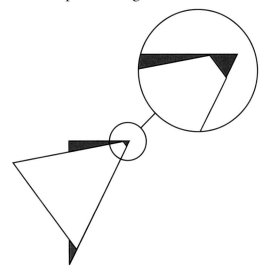

4. Assembly-line sew **with ¼" seam.**

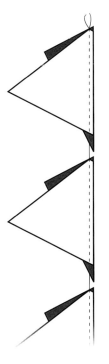

5. Set seam with Star Point on top. Open, and press seam toward Star Point.

6. Place remaining Star Points to right of Background triangles. Flip right sides together.

7. Line top tip of both triangles together. Assembly-line sew.

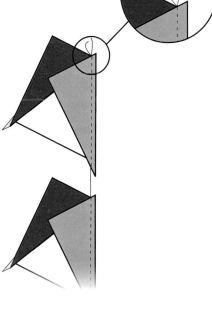

8. Set seams with Star Point on top. Open, and press seam toward Star Point.

Squaring Star Points

12" Finished Block

1. Place patch on small cutting mat.

2. Place Triangle in a Square Ruler on top of patch. **Line up green triangle lines with seams.**

6" Finished Block

1. Place patch on small cutting mat.

2. Place **2½" Fussy Cut Ruler** on top of patch. For ¼" seam, line up green dashed line with tip of Background triangle.

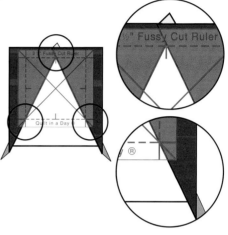

For seams ⅛" from bottom corners, line up green lines with seams.

3. Trim patch on four sides while rotating mat.

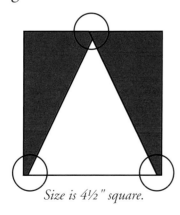

Size is 4½" square.

4. Seams are ¼" from top edge, and ⅛" from bottom corners.

3. Trim patch on four sides while rotating mat.

Size is 2½" square.

4. Seams are ¼" from top edge, and ⅛" from bottom corners.

Sewing Block Together

1. Lay out pieces.

2. Flip middle vertical row right sides together to left vertical row.

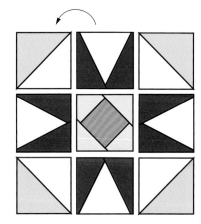

3. Assembly-line sew. Do not clip connecting threads. Open.

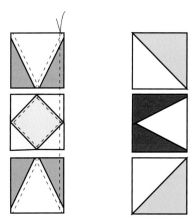

4. Flip right vertical row to middle vertical row.

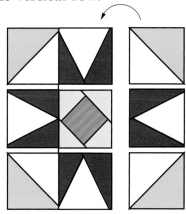

5. Assembly-line sew.

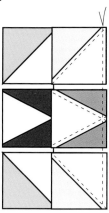

6. Do not clip connecting threads.

7. Turn block. Flip right vertical row to middle vertical row. Push seams away from Star Points, and lock. Sew.

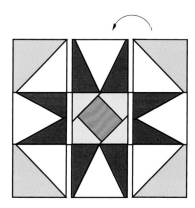

8. Repeat with remaining row.

9. Press just sewn seams away from center.

Dora's Delight Wallhanging

Teresa Varnes
Amie Potter
36" x 36"

Make four 12" finished blocks and four 6" finished blocks. Follow directions for blocks beginning on page 146. Setting illustrations begin on page 175. Substitute Dora's Delight blocks for Harvest Star blocks.

Make center of wallhanging with two different blocks.

Make two 12" blocks and two 6" blocks repeating center square fabric on corners.

Make two 12" blocks and two 6" blocks repeating triangle fabric on corners.

	Four 12" Finished Blocks	Four 6" Finished Blocks
Background	**1½ yds**	
Star Points	(2) 5" strips	(1) 3" strip
Corners	(1) 5" strip cut into (4) 5" x 10" rectangles	(1) 3" strip cut into (4) 3" x 6" rectangles
Outside Triangles	(1) 7" strip cut into (4) 7" squares	
Border	Cut on one diagonal (4) 4½" strips	
Floral Print	**¼ yd**	
Center Squares	(4) 3¼" squares	(4) 1⅞" squares
Corners	(2) 5" x 10" rectangles	(2) 3" x 6" rectangles
Green	**⅓ yd**	
Center Triangles	(8) 3½" squares	(8) 2¼" squares
Corners	(2) 5" x 10" rectangles	(2) 3" x 6" rectangles
Pink	**1 yd**	
Star Points	(2) 6" strips cut into (16) 3" x 6" rectangles	(1) 3⅝" strip cut into (16) 1⅞" x 3⅝" rectangles
Folded Border	(4) 1¼" strips	
Binding	(4) 3" strips	
Backing	**1¼ yds**	
Batting	**44" x 44"**	

North Star Block

The North Star Block hangs on the weathered gambrel roof barn at the Wheelock Farm in Kent, New York, owned by Chet and Audrey Wheelock. Chet had grown up on a farm, and after visiting her grandparents' farm as a girl, Audrey said she never wanted to marry a farmer. They married in 1952!

Since moving to the area in 1956, they have been partners in what began as tenant farming and grew into a three farm dairy and feed crop operation. Through the years, they raised a son and three daughters, who helped out with farm chores when needed. Now they spend their winter months in Florida, enjoying leisure time after many years of hard work.

When choosing a quilt design for their barn, they liked the patriotic colors of the North Star and the way those colors stood out from the background. Hanging the block in a diamond configuration utilizes the peak of the barn and gives their block a different look from others on the Western New York Country Barn Quilt Trail. Their area is often referred to as the "Black North", so the North Star seemed an appropriate choice. www.countrybarnquilttrail.com

photo –Dale Smalley

Home Art Studios out of Des Moines, Iowa is the source for this striking pattern dating back to the 30's.

The North Star block is also the logo for Barn Quilts of Grundy County, Iowa's original barn quilt project.

Visit www.grundycountyia.com and click on the Barn Quilt logo.

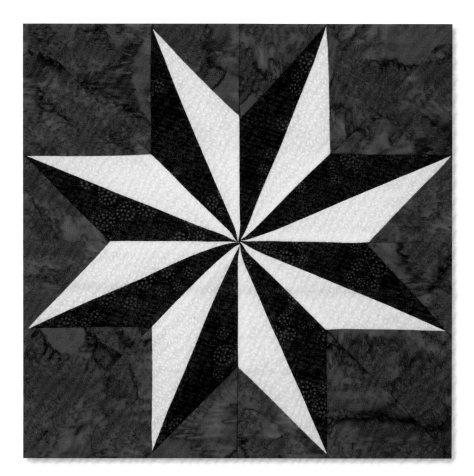

Skill Level – Challenging

Supplies for 12" Block
Kaleidoscope Ruler
Glow-Line Tape
6½" Fussy Cut Ruler
6½" Triangle Square Up Ruler
Small Cutting Mat

Supplies for 6" Block
Kaleidoscope Ruler
Glow-Line Tape
3½" Fussy Cut Ruler
Small Cutting Mat

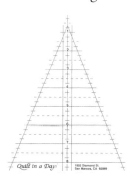

Kaleidoscope Ruler

Glow-Line Tape

	12" Finished Block	6" Finished Block
Background		
Large Squares	(4) 4¾" squares	(4) 2⅞" squares
Small Squares	(4) 3¾" squares	(4) 2⅜" squares
Red		
Diamonds	(4) 2" x 20"	(2) 1¼" x 20"
	or (2) 2" x 40"	or (1) 1¼" x 40"
Background		
Diamonds	(4) 2" x 20"	(2) 1¼" x 20"
	or (2) 2" x 40"	or (1) 1¼" x 40"

Sewing Diamond Strips

1. Set machine for ¼" seam. **Do not use a scant ¼" seam.**

2. Lay out strips with red on right, and Background on left.

12" Block	6" Block
2" strips	1¼" strips

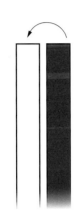

3. Sew strips together with ¼" seam.

4. Set seam with red on top. Open, and press toward red.

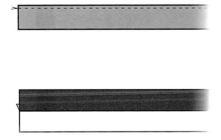

5. Trim selvage edge. Cut into eight pieces.

12" Block	6" Block
8" pieces	4¾" pieces

6. Fold in half right sides together, and line up seams. Press fold.

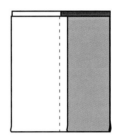

Cutting Eight Diamonds

1. Place Kaleidoscope Ruler wrong side up. Place strip of Glow-line tape under designated measurement.

12" Block	6" Block
3⅞" measurement	2¼" measurement

2. Place Kaleidoscope Ruler on folded Diamond strip with marked measurement on fold. Line up center line with seam.

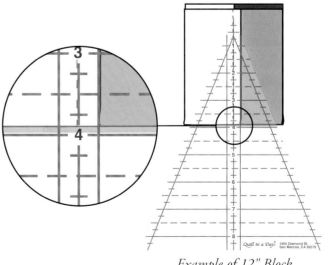

Example of 12" Block

3. Cut eight Diamonds.

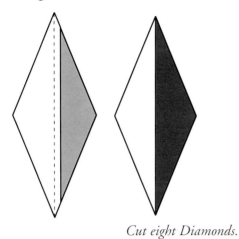

Cut eight Diamonds.

4. Open and check for sharp points.

 **Sewing Four Quarters**

1. Lay out pair of Diamonds. Stack four sets.

2. Cut Large Squares in half on one diagonal.

12" Block	6" Block
4¾" squares	2⅞" squares

3. Place with Diamonds.

4. Cut Small Squares in half on one diagonal.

12" Block	6" Block
3¾" squares	2⅜" squares

5. Place with Diamonds.

6. Divide into Left Half and Right Half.

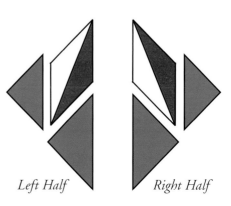

Left Half   *Right Half*

Sewing Left Half

1. Separate out left half.

2. Flip Diamond right sides together to Small Triangle on left.

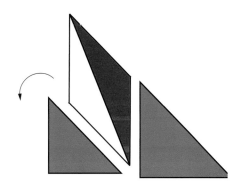

3. Let ⅜" tip hang over on top edge. Assembly-line sew.

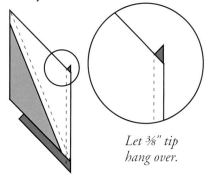

Let ⅜" tip hang over.

4. Set seam with Small Triangle on top.

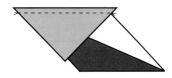

5. Open, and press toward Small Triangle. Using ruler as a straight edge, trim tips.

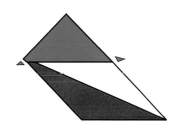

6. Place with Large Triangles

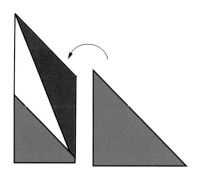

7. Flip Large Triangle right sides together to patch. Let ⅜" tip hang over on top edge.

8. Assembly-line sew.

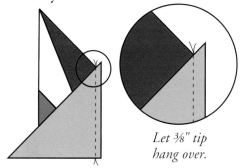

Let ⅜" tip hang over.

9. Set seam with Large Triangle on top.

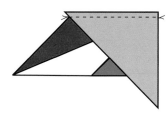

10. Open, and press toward Large Triangle. Trim tip.

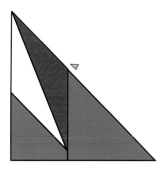

Sewing Right Half

1. Lay out Right Half.

2. Flip Diamond right sides together to Large Triangle on left.

3. Let ⅜" tip hang over on top edge. Assembly-line sew.

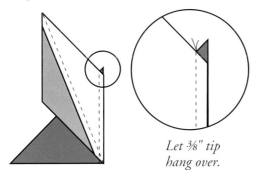

Let ⅜" tip hang over.

4. Set seam with Large Triangle on top.

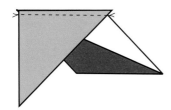

5. Open, and press toward Large Triangle. Trim tips.

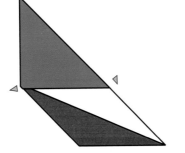

6. Place with Small Triangles.

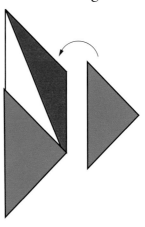

7. Flip Small Triangle right sides together to patch. Let ⅜" tips hang over on both edges.

8. Assembly-line sew.

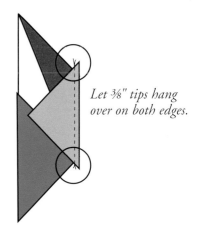

Let ⅜" tips hang over on both edges.

9. Set seam with Small Triangle on top.

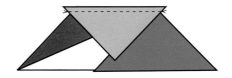

10. Open, and press toward Small Triangle. Trim tips.

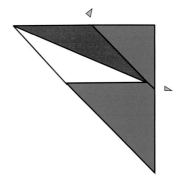

Sewing Quarters Together

1. Lay out Left and Right patches.

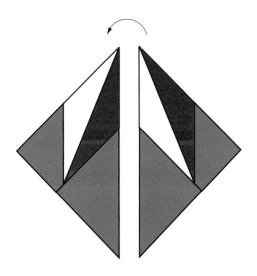

2. Flip right sides together. Lock Diamonds. Match and pin Diamond seams and ends together. Sew.

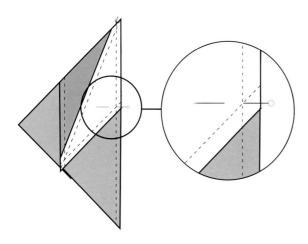

3. Set seam with stitches across top, open, and press.

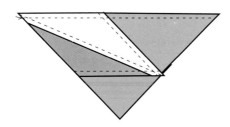

4. Square patch with ruler.

12" Block	6" Block
6½" Fussy Cut Ruler or 6½" Triangle Square Up Ruler	3½" Fussy Cut Ruler

Seam must be at least a ¼". Seam may "float."

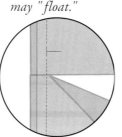

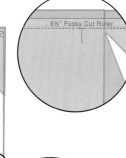

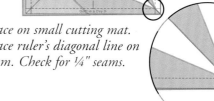

Place on small cutting mat. Place ruler's diagonal line on seam. Check for ¼" seams.

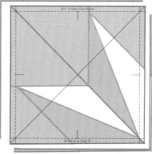

Seam must be ¼".

Using Fussy Cut Ruler, rotate mat, trim block on four sides.

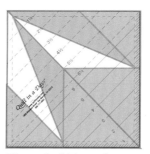

Using 6½" Triangle Square Up Ruler

Seam is a ¼".

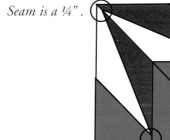

Seam "floats."

Sewing Block Together

1. Lay out four patches.

2. Flip vertical row of patches on right to vertical rows of patches on left, right sides together. Put needle in fabric and presser foot down to avoid jamming. Start out sewing slowly.

3. Lock seams, and assembly-line sew. Do not clip connecting thread.

4. Turn. Flip vertical row on right to vertical row on left.

5. Lock center seams, pushing top seam up, and underneath seam down.

6. Sew.

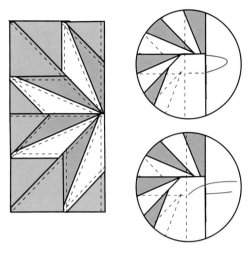

7. Clip connecting thread in center and remove three straight stitches in vertical seam allowance. See red thread.

8. Turn block over and remove remaining three straight stitches.

9. Place on pressing mat wrong side up. Push top vertical seam to right, and bottom vertical seam to left. Center will pop open and make a little pinwheel.

10. Press center flat with your finger. Press so seams swirl around center clockwise.

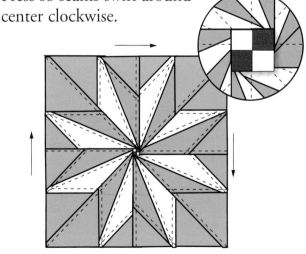

11. Measure.

12" Block	6" Block
12½"	6½"

Harvest Star Block

The Harvest Star block, mounted on Harold and Sue Peyton's Corncrib, was the first barn quilt to go up in Sac County, Iowa. History dates the block to the late 1890s and was published by the Ladies Art Company, credited to be the first mail order quilt pattern company.

The corncrib was built in 1948 on property owned by Peyton ancestors since 1891. The price back then was $23 per acre. Current owner Harold Peyton is the fourth generation to farm this land east of Sac County.

Eleanor traveled to this site in September 2009 to attend Sac County Quilt-A-Fair, and enjoyed good old fashioned Iowa hospitality extended by the Peyton family. www.barnquilts.com

At harvest time, neighbors met at dusk in a barn for a Corn Husking Party. Two teams sat around a long pile of corn. As the contest began, fingers moved quickly and dozens of ears hit the door. Occasionally, when a young man found a red ear in his corn, he kissed a girl of his choice. When a girl found a red ear, she handed it to her favorite young man for a kiss. Sometimes, an unattached young man hide a red ear in his pocket before going "a husking." The huskers talked, joked, and sang folk songs as they hurried to finish their work.

photo – Brian Stuetel

PEYTON, INC.
FINE IOWA PORK AND BEEF

Skill Level – Challenging

Supplies for 12" Block
   12½" Square Up Ruler
   6½" Triangle Square Up Ruler
   6" Square Up Ruler
   Glow-Line™ Tape

Supplies for 6" Block
   6½" Triangle Square Up Ruler
   6" Square Up Ruler
   Glow-Line™ Tape

6" Square Up Ruler

Glow-Line™ Tape

	12" Finished Block	6" Finished Block
Background		
Light Diamond	(1) 1¾" x 42" strip	(1) 1⅛" x 42" strip
Red		
Dark Diamond	(1) 1¾" x 42" strip	(1) 1⅛" x 42" strip
Yellow		
Corner Squares	(4) 4⅜" squares	(4) 2½" squares
Side Triangles	(1) 2¼" strip	(1) 1⅜" x 18" strip
Blue		
Corner Triangles	(4) 2¼" squares	(4) 1⅜" squares
Side Triangles	(1) 2" strip cut into	(1) 1⅜" x 9" strip cut into
	(4) 2" x 3½"	(4) 1⅜" x 2"

Making Diamonds

Sew with ¼" seam. Do not sew with a scant ¼".

1. Lay out two Diamond strips, with Dark on the right.

12" Block	6" Block
1¾" x 42"	1⅛" x 42"

2. Flip Dark strip right sides together to Light strip, and sew length of strip. **Do not sew with a scant ¼" seam.**

3. Set seam with Dark on top, open, and press toward Dark.

4. **Check width of two sewn together strips.** Trim or resew if necessary.

Use 6" Square Up Ruler.

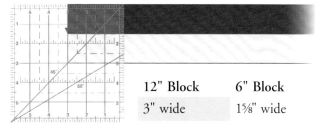

12" Block	6" Block
3" wide	1⅝" wide

Right Handed Cutters Only

1. Place strips on cutting mat, right side up, with red across top.

2. Place 6" Square Up Ruler on left end of strip. Line up 45° line across top of strip.

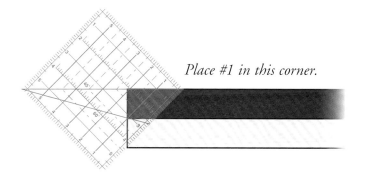

Place #1 in this corner.

3. Cut off corner of strip on 45° angle.

4. Slide ruler to right, keeping 45° angle across top of strip. Line up ruler's designated line on cut edge. Cut again.

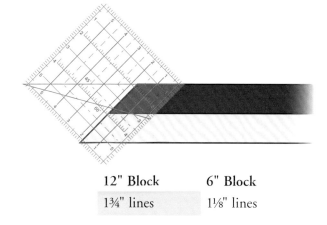

12" Block	6" Block
1¾" lines	1⅛" lines

Left Handed Cutters Only

Right and Left Handed Cutters

1. **Continue to cut a total of sixteen diamonds.**

2. Stack Diamonds in eight pairs. Flip top Diamond on right to top Diamond on left.

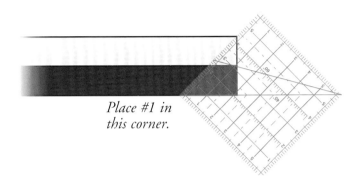

Place #1 in this corner.

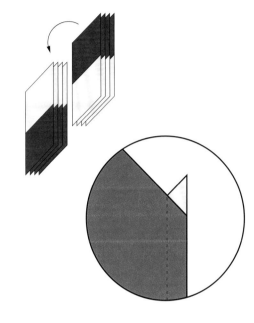

3. Cut off corner of strip on 45° angle.

4. Slide ruler to left, keeping 45° angle across bottom of strip. Line up ruler's designated line on cut edge. Cut again.

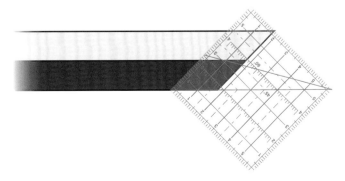

3. Line up top and bottom with ¼" to ⅜" tips hanging over.

4. Hold pair up to light, and pin where seams cross. This is the match point.

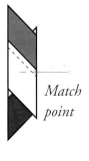

Match point

5. Assembly-line sew, pulling pin out of seam just before stitching match point.

12" Block	6" Block
1¾" lines	1⅛" lines

6. Place on pressing mat, and set seam.

7. Open, and press.

8. Trim tip.

Sewing Pairs of Diamonds Together

1. Divide diamonds into two stacks of four each. **For locking seams, turn diamonds so seams go in opposite directions.**

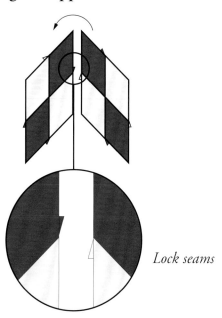

Lock seams

2. Flip first diamond on right onto first diamond on left. Lock seams.

3. With marking pencil and ruler, lightly draw lines ¼" in from bottom edge. Place a dot where lines intersect. Pin through dot.

 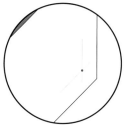

4. Sew diamonds together from top point to dot ¼" from edge. Do not backstitch. Sew all diamonds together.

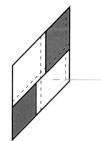 

5. **Set seam** with just sewn stitching across top.

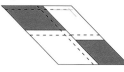

6. Open, and gently press toward stitching.

7. Place 6" Ruler's diagonal line on seam. Trim tip.

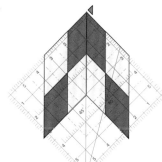

8. Set aside.

Making Corner Squares

1. Turn blue squares for Corner Triangles wrong side up. Draw diagonal line.

12" Block	6" Block
2¼" squares	1⅜" squares

2. Place one blue square on corner of one yellow square, right sides together.

12" Block	6" Block
4⅜" square	2½" square

3. Sew on line.

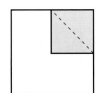

4. Trim ¼" from line.

5. Set seam with blue on top, open and press toward blue.

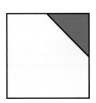

 ## Sewing Corners to Diamonds

1. Turn four Corner Squares wrong side up.

2. With a sharp marking pencil, place a small dot ¼" in on blue corner of each square.

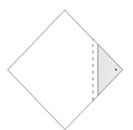

3. Place Diamond right side up. Place Corner Square wrong side up.

4. Push pin through marked dot on Corner into dot on Diamond.

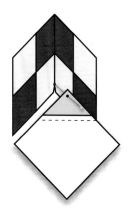 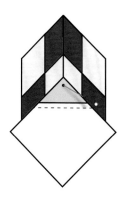

5. Line up sides of Corner and Diamond. **Match Triangle and Diamond seams.**

6. Turn. Sew from pin to end of square. Remove pin.

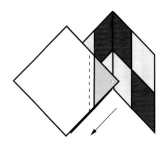 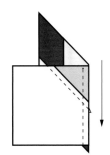

7. Swing Corner to second side of Diamond and line up raw edges. **Match Corner and Diamond seams.** Sew from dot to edge from Diamond side.

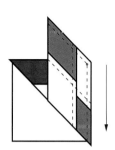

8. Place on pressing mat right side up.

9. Press seams away from Corner square.

10. Line up 6" Square Up Ruler with straight sides, and trim tips.

11. Repeat on remaining Corners.

12. Check on wrong side.

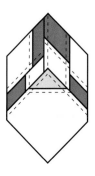

Sewing Star Together

1. Lay out Star.

2. Flip right half of Star onto left half of Star.

3. **Lock center seams.** Mark dots ¼" in on top and bottom, and pin.

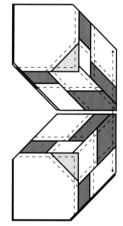

Match seams.

Do not clip connecting thread.

Match seams.

4. Sew together with ¼" seam, beginning and ending on dot ¼" in from edge. Do not clip center connecting thread.

5. Open and turn. Flip right sides together. Mark dots ¼" in on top and bottom, and pin. Sew remaining row.

6. At connecting thread, push top seam up, and underneath seam down.

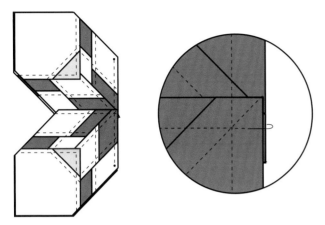

7. Clip connecting thread, and remove straight stitches in seam on both sides.

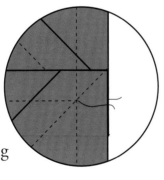

8. Lay block flat wrong side up.

9. Open center and press flat, swirling seams around center.

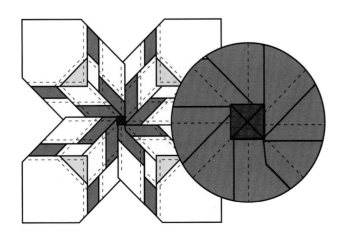

 ## Making Side Triangles

1. Turn 6½" Triangle Square Up Ruler wrong side up

2. Place Glow-Line™ tape below designated line.

12" Block	6" Block
5" line	3" line

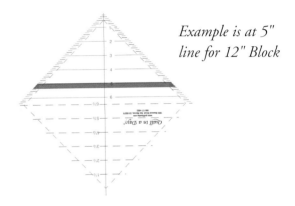

Example is at 5" line for 12" Block

3. Place Side Triangle strip right side up on cutting mat.

12" Block	6" Block
2¼" strip	1⅜" x 18" strip

4. Using 6½" Triangle Square Up Ruler, place designated line on bottom of strip, and cut four Trapezoid shapes.

12" Block	6" Block
5" line	3" line

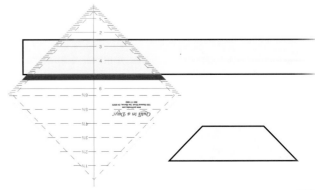

5. Center yellow trapezoid right sides together to blue rectangle, and assembly-line sew. *Rectangle is cut into triangle.*

12" Block	6" Block
2" x 3½"	1⅜" x 2"

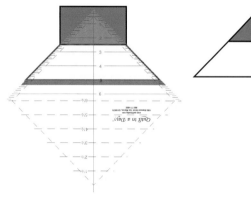

6. Set seam with blue rectangle on top, open and press toward blue rectangle.

7. Place designated line on 6½" Triangle Square Up Ruler across bottom of patch, and trim excess.

12" Block	6" Block
5" line	3" line

Sewing Side Triangles to Star

1. Turn Side Triangles wrong side up.

2. With a marking pencil, place dot in corner of triangle ¼" in from outside edge.

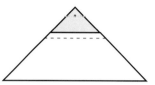

3. Working on one side at a time, pin and lock seam. Sew triangle into side, stitching from ¼" dot to outside edge.

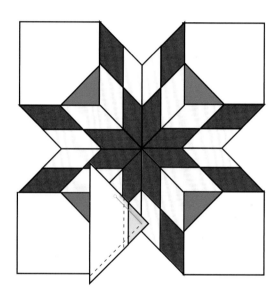

4. Flip and sew other side of triangle onto other side.

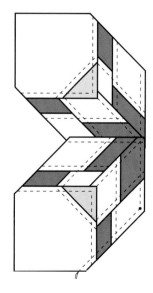

5. Press seams toward triangle.

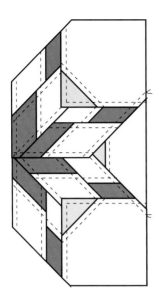

6. Repeat with remaining Side Triangles.

7. Square block, allowing **at least a ¼"
seam** from points of Star.

8. Measure and record in box.

12" Finished Block	6" Finished Block
12½" is ideal size	*6½" is ideal size*

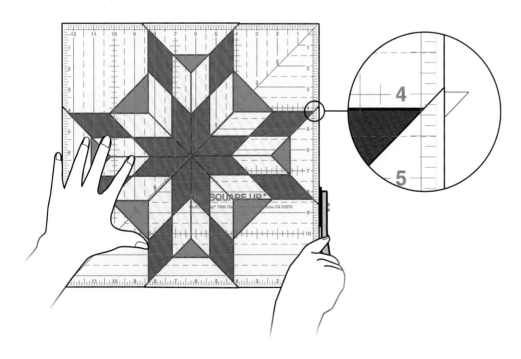

12" Finished Block	6" Finished Block
Square to 12½" with 12½" Square Up Ruler	Square to 6½" with 6½" Triangle Square Up Ruler

Harvest Star Wallhanging

Four 12" Finished Blocks and
Four 6" Finished Blocks

Any four 12" finished blocks and matching
6" finished blocks can be sewn together in
this setting.

Teresa Varnes
Amie Potter
37" x 37"

	Four 12" Finished Blocks	Four 6" Finished Blocks
Background	³⁄₈ yd	
Light Diamond	(4) 1¾" x 42" strips	(4) 1⅛" x 42" strips
Red	³⁄₈ yd	
Dark Diamond	(4) 1¾" x 42" strips	(4) 1⅛" x 42" strips
Yellow	1½ yds	
Corner Squares	(2) 4⅜" strips cut into (16) 4⅜" squares	(1) 2½" strip cut into (16) 2½" squares
Side Triangles	(3) 2¼" strips	(2) 1⅜" strips
Triangles	(1) 7" strip cut into (4) 7" squares *(cut on one diagonal)*	
Border	(4) 4½" strips	
Blue	⅞ yds	
Corner Triangles	(1) 2¼" strip cut into (16) 2¼" squares	(1) 1⅜" strip cut into (16) 1⅜" squares
Side Triangles	(2) 2" strips cut into (16) 2" x 3½" rectangles	(1) 1⅜" strip cut into (16) 1⅜" x 2" rectangles
Folded Border	(4) 1¼" strips	
Binding	(4) 3" strips	
Backing	1¼ yds	
Batting	45" x 45"	

Making Stars

1. Make four 12" finished size Stars, and four 6" finished size Stars.

2. Sew four 12" Stars together in two by two layout.

Adding Triangles to Corner Stars

1. Stack four 6" Stars with four triangles cut from 7" yellow squares.

2. Flip Star to triangle right sides together, matching top and right edges. Assembly-line sew.

3. Press seam toward triangles. Trim tips.

4. Sew remaining triangles.

5. Press seams toward triangles, carefully avoiding long bias edge.

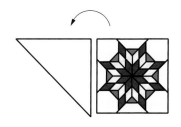

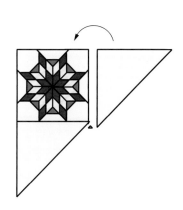

Adding Borders to Corner Stars

1. Fold Folded Border 1¼" strip in half lengthwise **wrong sides together**. Press.

2. Lay Folded Border on right side of 4½" border, matching raw edges. Sew ⅛" from raw edges.

3. Lay out Border and Star piece. Measure down 5½" from end of Border.

4. Flip Star to Border. Start sewing ¼" in from edge of Star corner in order to miter borders. See dot on Star block.

5. Open and **press seam toward Star and Folded Border toward 4½" Border**. Lay a 6" x 24" ruler along long edge of triangle, lining up 45° line on ruler. Trim off excess.

6. Use 4½" Border excess for other side of Star piece. Measure 5½" from end of border. Pin often from dot on block to end of triangle. Sew from triangle toward block. Leave ¼" of block free where Borders meet.

7. Open and press seam toward Star.

8. Place ruler across edge of triangle with 45° on edge. Trim off excess border.

9. Repeat with remaining three corner stars.

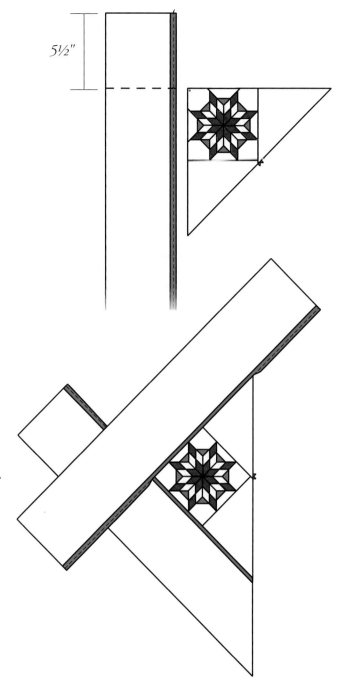

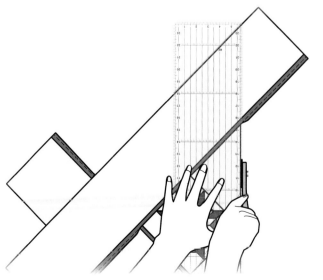

Mitering Corners

1. Fold corner diagonally right sides together. Match Border and Folded Border strips, right sides together.

2. Fingerpress seam away from Border so stitching shows.

3. Line 45° angle on 6" x 24" ruler with seam of Border.

4. Following quilt fold, draw a diagonal line on Border extension.

5. Starting exactly at the ¼" point, sew on drawn line.

6. Open quilt and check to see if pieces line up. Sew again if necessary.

7. Repeat with remaining corners. Trim seams to ¼". Press open.

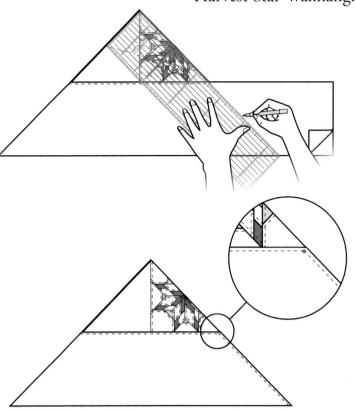

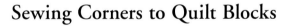

Sewing Corners to Quilt Blocks

1. Lay out corner pieces next to quilt top.

2. Center each corner by matching center seams of quilt with point of corner Star.

3. Pin bias edge to quilt on opposite corners. Sew carefully without stretching bias edge. Fold out. Press seam toward Border. Trim tips.

4. Sew on remaining two sides.

5. Press seam toward border.

6. Quilt and bind.

Sewing Top Together

Making American Barns Panel (Optional)

1. Trace letters found on pattern sheet onto paper side of paper backed fusible web. There are two sizes, one for the Large Barn Quilt and one for the Small Barn Quilt.

Large Barn Quilt	Small Barn Quilt
3½" strips	3" strips

2. Place black letter fabric wrong side up on pressing mat. Center rough side of fusible letters on wrong side of fabric.

3. Fuse in place for two seconds. Allow pieces to cool.

4. Using sharp scissors, cut out each letter on the line.

5. Peel off paper backing by running your fingernail across the edge of the paper, or scratch the paper with a pin.

6. Center letters on Background rectangle.

Large Barn Quilt	Small Barn Quilt
8½" x 26½"	5½" x 18½"

7. Fuse letters in place for 8-10 seconds.

8. Satin stitch around letters with matching thread.

If you find a local quilt shop who will embroider the panel professionally, send them ⅓ yd Background so they have excess to put it in their machine. Trim to size after stitching is completed.

Large Barn Quilt

Eleanor Burns
Amie Potter
70" x 70"

Lattice measurements are given based on an accurate ¼" seam allowance. However, your measurements may be different based on your personal seam allowance.

This fabric is included in the yardage chart on page 14.
Cut these strips to finish your quilt.

Background	**2½ yds**
Lattice	(15) 2½" strips
Checkerboard	(12) 2½" strips
Chicken Blocks	(1) 6½" strip cut into
	(4) 6½" squares
Optional Letter Panel	(1) 8½" x 26½"

Black	**1½ yds**
Letters	(1) 3½" strip
First Border	(6) 1½" strips
Chicken Blocks	(1) 6" strip cut into
	(4) 6" squares
Binding	(8) 3" strips

Red	**1 yd**
Checkerboard	(12) 2½" strips
Chicken Blocks	(1) 2½" x 8" strip

Backing	**4¾ yds**
Batting	**80" x 80"**

Paper Backed Fusible Web ¼ yd

Optional Letters	(2) 3½" strips

Sewing Large Barn Quilt Together

1. Select blocks. You need:

    one 18½" x 26½" Monitor Barn

    four 12½" Barns

    eight 12½" Pieced Blocks

    three 6½" Pieced Blocks
    or one 8½" x 26½" Letter Panel

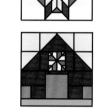

2. Measure and trim or resew blocks.

3. **Barns:** Lay out 12½" Barns in each corner and Monitor Barn with Windmill in upper center.

4. Place three 6½" blocks under Monitor Barn, or Letter Panel above Monitor Barn.

5. Place eight remaining 12½" blocks around outside edges between 12½" Barn blocks.

Cutting Lattice Between Blocks

1. Count out three 2½" selvage to selvage Background strips.

2. Cut into eight 2½" x 12½" strips for between 12½" blocks.

Sewing Rows Together

Sew top together with a ¼" seam. Do not use a scant ¼".

1. **Top and Bottom Rows:** Sew each row together with four 12½" blocks and three 2½" x 12½" Lattice. Press seams toward Lattice. Measure length of row. Ideal length should be 54½".

Cutting and Sewing Short Lattice and Lattice Between 6½" Blocks

1. Count out three 2½" selvage to selvage Background strips.

2. Cut into three 2½" x 28" strips for Short Lattice.

3. Cut left-overs from 2½" strips into four 2½" x 6½" strips for between 6½" blocks.

4. **Row under Monitor Barn and Windmill:** Sew together with three 6½" blocks and four 2½" x 6½" Lattice strips. Press seams toward Lattice.

5. Measure length of row. Ideal length should be 26½".

6. Cut three Short Lattice to same size, ideally 26½".

7. Sew Monitor Barn with Windmill to 6½" block row with 2½" x 26½" Lattice between the two. Press seams toward Lattice.

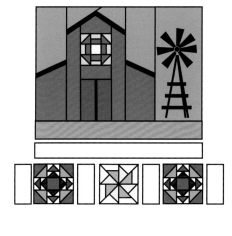

Optional Letter Row

1. Sew 8½" x 26½" Letter Panel to top of Barn.

2. Press seam toward Letter Panel.

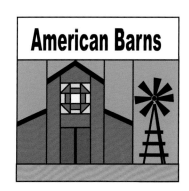

Sewing Sides Together

1. Sew together with 12½" blocks and 2½" x 12½" Lattice. Press seams toward Lattice. Measure length of row. Ideal length should be 26½".

2. Sew 2½" x 26½" Lattice to sides, and press toward Lattice.

3. Sew two sides to Monitor Barn grouping.

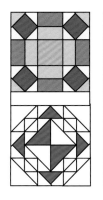 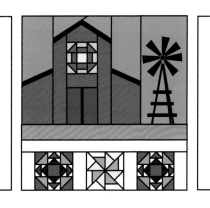 

Cutting and Sewing Long Lattice

1. Count out three 2½" selvage to selvage Background strips.

2. Cut strips in half into six 2½" x 20" strips.

3. Piece 2½" x 20" strips to the ends of remaining six 2½" x 40" strips.

4. Measure length of rows. Ideal length should be 54½".

5. Cut four 2½" x 60" Lattice strips into your measurement.

6. Sew three sections together with four 2½" x 54½" Long Lattice. Press seams toward Lattice.

7. Measure two sides, and find average length, ideally 58½".

8. Cut 2½" Lattice to your average length. Sew to sides. Press seams toward Lattice.

9. Turn to page 191 for **Sewing First Border for All Tops.**

Extra Long Barn Quilt

Select this setting if you made all the 12½" and 18" Monitor Barn blocks and want a longer quilt. This fabric is included in the yardage chart on page 14. Cut these strips to finish your quilt.

Teresa Varnes
Amie Potter
72" x 84"

Lattice measurements are given based on an accurate ¼" seam allowance. However, your measurements may be different based on your personal seam allowance.

This fabric is included in the yardage chart on page 14.
Cut these strips to finish your quilt.

Background	**3 yds**
Lattice	(15) 2½" strips
Top and Bottom Lattice	(3) 1½" strips
Checkerboard	(15) 2½" strips
Chicken Blocks	(1) 6½" strip cut into (4) 6½" squares
Optional Letter Panel	(1) 8½" x 26½"

Black	**1¾ yds**
Optional Letters	(1) 3½" strip
First Border	(7) 2½" strips
Chicken Blocks	(1) 6" strip cut into (4) 6" squares
Binding	(9) 3" strips

Red	**1¼ yds**
Checkerboard	(15) 2½" strips
Chicken Blocks	(1) 2½" x 8" strip

Backing	5¼ yds
Batting	86" x 98"

Paper Backed Fusible Web ¼ yd

Optional Letters	(2) 3½" strips

Sewing Extra Long Barn Quilt Together

1. Select blocks. You need:

   one 18½" x 26½" Monitor Barn

   four 12½" Barns

   twelve 12½" Pieced Blocks

   three 6½" Pieced Blocks
   or one 8½" x 26½" Letter Panel

2. Measure and trim or resew blocks if necessary.

3. **Barns:** Lay out Barns with a 12½" block in each corner and Monitor Barn with Windmill in upper center.

4. Place three 6½" blocks under Monitor Barn with Windmill, or Letter Panel above Monitor Barn.

5. Place twelve remaining 12½" blocks in your layout.

Cutting Lattice Between Blocks

1. Count out four 2½" selvage to selvage Background strips.

2. Cut into eleven 2½" x 12½" strips for between 12½" blocks.

Sewing Rows Together

Sew top together with a ¼" seam.
Do not use a scant ¼".

1. **Top, Fourth, and Bottom Rows:** Sew each row together with four 12½" blocks and three 2½" x 12½" Lattice. Press seams toward Lattice. Measure length of row. Ideal length should be 54½".

Cutting and Sewing Short Lattice and Lattice Between 6½" Blocks

1. Count out three 2½" selvage to selvage Background strips.

2. Cut into three 2½" x 28" strips for Short Lattice.

3. Cut left-overs from 2½" strips into four 2½" x 6½" strips for between 6½" blocks.

4. **Row under Monitor Barn and Windmill:** Sew together with three 6½" blocks and four 2½" x 6½" Lattice strips. Press seams toward Lattice.

5. Measure length of row. Ideal length should be 26½".

6. Cut three Short Lattice to same size, ideally 26½".

7. Sew Monitor Barn with Windmill to 6½" block row with 2½" x 26½" Lattice between the two. Press seams toward Lattice.

Optional Letter Row

1. Sew 8½" x 26½" Letter Panel to top of Barn.

2. Press seam toward Letter Panel.

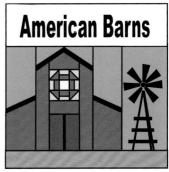

Sewing Sides Together

1. Sew together with 12½" blocks and 2½" x 12½" Lattice. Press seams toward Lattice. Measure length of row. Ideal length should be 26½".

2. Sew 2½" x 26½" Lattice to sides, and press toward Lattice.

3. Sew two sides to Monitor Barn grouping.

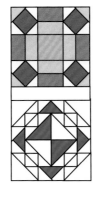

Cutting and Sewing Long Inside Lattice

1. Count out two 2½" selvage to selvage Background strips.

2. Cut three strips in half into four 2½" x 20" strips. Set one half aside.

3. Piece 2½" x 20" strips to ends of three 2½" x 40" strips.

4. Measure length of Barn row. Ideal length should be 54½".

5. Cut three 2½" x 60" Lattice strips into your measurement.

6. **Sew three inside sections together with 2½" Lattice.** Press seams toward Lattice.

Cutting and Sewing Top and Bottom Lattice

1. Count out three **1½" selvage to selvage Background strips.**

2. Cut one strip in half and piece half strips to ends of two 1½" x 40" strips.

3. **Sew to top and bottom,** and press toward Lattice.

Cutting and Sewing Side Lattice

1. Piece four 2½" x 40" strips together into two long strips.

2. Measure sides. Ideal length should be 70½". Cut to your measurement and sew to sides. Press toward Lattice.

3. Turn to page 191 for **Sewing First Border to All Quilts.**

Small Barn Quilt

Teresa Varnes
Amie Potter
40" x 40"

Lattice measurements are given based on an accurate ¼" seam allowance. However, your measurements may be different based on your personal seam allowance.

This fabric is included in the yardage chart on page 14. Cut these strips to finish your quilt.

Background	**1¼ yds**
	(1) 3½" strip cut into
Solid Squares	(2) 3½" squares
Rectangles	(4) 2" x 3½" rectangles
Lattice	(8) 1½" strips
	cut (2) into
	(12) 1½" x 6½" strips
Block Lattice	
Letter Panel	(1) 5½" x 18½"
	(1) 1" strip cut into
	(2) 1" x 17½" strips
Sides of Barn	
Checkerboard	(9) 1½" strips

Black	**⅝ yd**
Letters	(1) 3" strip
First Border	(4) 1" strips
Binding	(4) 2½" strips

Red	**½ yd**
Checkerboard	(9) 1½" strips

Backing	**2½ yds**
Batting	**48" x 48"**
Paper Backed Fusible Web	**¼ yd**
	(2) 3" strips

Cutting for Five Mini Stars
Make one 3" Star for 3" x 6" block and four 3" Stars for Corners.

Background	**¼ yd**
Points	(5) 4½" squares
Centers	(5) 2" squares

Blue	**¼ yd**
Points	(5) 3" squares
Corners	(20) 1¼" squares

Sewing Five 3" Mini Stars

Make one 3" Star for 3" x 6" block
and four 3" Stars for Corners.

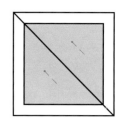

1. Center blue 3" squares right sides together to five Background 4½" squares. Draw a diagonal line.

2. Make Geese following directions beginning on page 26.

3. Use Mini Geese Ruler Two and square Geese to ¾" x 1½" finished size. Size with seams included is 1¼" x 2".

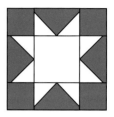

4. Sew Stars together following directions on pages 125 and 126.

Making Four 3" x 6" Blocks

1. Make three additional 3" finished size blocks, or 3½" square including seams.

 Hole in the Barn Door - page 31   Flying Kite - page 133

 End of the Day - page 43   One Mini Star from Americana Star - use one of five

2. Select any two 3½" blocks. Sew 2" x 3½" Background rectangles to two sides.

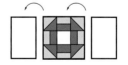 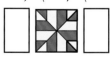

3. Set seams with Background on top, open, and press seams toward Background.

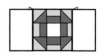 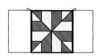

4. Select two "fussy cut" animals approximately 2½" tall. Center and fuse to 3½" Background squares, and stitch around outside edges.

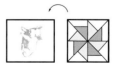

5. Sew "fussy cut" animal squares to two 3½" pieced blocks. Press seams toward Background squares.

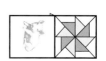 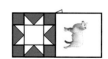

Sewing Small Barn Quilt Together

1. Select blocks. You need:

   one 12½" x 18½" Monitor Barn with Windmill

   one 5½" x 18½" Letter Panel or
   four additional 3½" Pieced Blocks

   four 6½" Barns

   eight 6½" Pieced Blocks

   four 3½" x 6½" Rectangular Blocks

2. Measure and trim or resew blocks if necessary.

3. **Barns:** Lay out 6½" Barn blocks in each corner and 12½" Monitor Barn with Windmill in center.

4. **Sides:** Place two 6½" blocks and one 3½" x 6½" block on each side.

5. **Top and Bottom Rows:** Place two 6½" blocks and one 3½" x 6½" block between Barn blocks in each row.

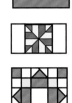

Optional Replacement for Letter Panel

1. In place of Letter Panel, make four additional 3" finished size blocks, or 3½" fussy cuts such as animals.

2. Sew four 3½" blocks together with 1½" x 3½" Lattice between blocks.

3. Sew 2" x 3½" Lattice on both ends.

4. Press seams toward Background.

5. Sew 1½" x 18½" Lattice to top and bottom.

6. Press seams toward Background.

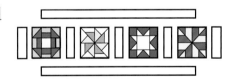
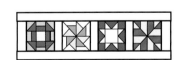

Sewing Rows Together

Sew top together with a ¼" seam. Do not use a scant ¼".

1. **Top and Bottom Rows:** Sew each row together with four 6½" blocks, one 3½" x 6½" block, and four 1½" x 6½" Lattice. Press seams toward Lattice. Measure length of row. Ideal length should be 31½".

2. **Side Rows:** Sew each row together with two 6½" blocks, one 3½" x 6½" block, and two 1½" x 6½" Lattice. Press seams toward Lattice. Measure length of row. Ideal length should be 17½".

3. **Monitor Barn and Windmill:** Sew 5½" x 18½" Letter Panel to Monitor Barn and Windmill. Press seams toward Lattice.

4. Sew **1" x 17½" Lattice** between Barn and side rows. Press seams toward 1" Lattice.

5. Measure length of row. Ideal length should be 31½".

6. Cut four 1½" x 40" Lattice strips into your measurement.

7. Sew three sections together with four 1½" x 31½" Lattice. Press seams toward Lattice.

8. Measure two sides, and find average length, ideally 33½".

9. Sew 1½" x 33½" Lattice to sides. Press toward Lattice.

Sewing First Border for All Quilts

If necessary, piece strips together.

1. Sew First Border to top and bottom. Press seams toward First Border. Trim even with quilt top.

Large Barn Quilt	Small Barn Quilt	Extra Long Barn Quilt
1½" strips	1" strips	2½" strips

2. Sew First Border to sides. Press seams toward First Border. Trim even with quilt top.

191

Making Checkerboard Border

1. Stack selvage to selvage strips. Place this many in each stack.

Large Barn Quilt	Small Barn Quilt	Extra Long Quilt
(4) 2½" strips	(3) 1½" strips	(5) 2½" strips

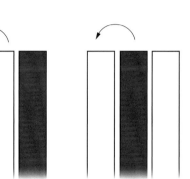

2. Assembly-line sew first two strips of each set.

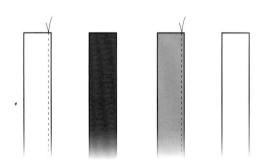

3. Set seams with red on top. Open, and press seams toward red.

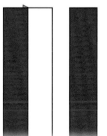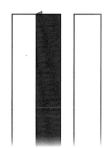

4. Sew remaining strips.

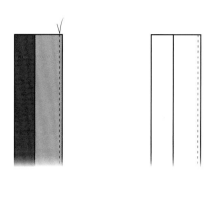

5. Press seams toward red.

Cutting Strips into Pairs

1. Place one red/white/red strip set on cutting mat, right side up.

2. Place one white/red/white strip set right sides together to first strip.

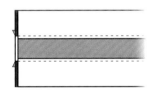

3. Layer cut into pairs with Shape Cut or ruler and rotary cutter.

Large Barn Quilt	Small Barn Quilt	Extra Long Quilt
(60) 2½" pairs	(68) 1½" pairs	(67) 2½" pairs

4. Repeat with all strip sets. Stack pairs right sides together.

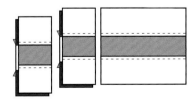

5. Lock seams and assembly-line sew. Do not cut apart.

6. Set seams in a chain, open, and cut apart.

7. Divide into four stacks.

Large Barn Quilt	Small Barn Quilt	Extra Long Quilt
(15) 2½" pairs each	(17) 1½" pairs each	(15) 2½" pairs plus one for top and bottom (18) 2½" pairs plus one for each side

8. Assembly-line sew each stack together. Make four sets the same length for Large and Small Barn Quilts.

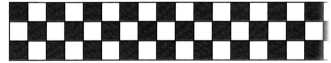

Extra Long Barn Quilt: Make two sets of 37 for sides. Make two sets of 31 for Top and Bottom.

9. Press seams in one direction.

10. Check length for ideal measurement.

Large Barn Quilt	Small Barn Quilt	Extra Long Quilt
60½" in length	34½" in length	62½" length for top and bottom 74½" length for each side

Making Chicken and Rooster Applique for Large Barn Quilts

1. Trace small hens and small roosters on paper side of paper back fusible web with permanent marking pen, leaving at least ½" between shapes. Trace two sets of hens, and two sets of roosters.

2. Rough cut around shapes.

3. Turn black and red fabrics wrong side up and press.

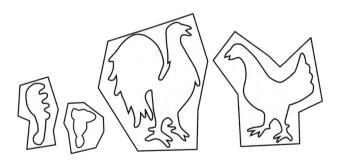

4. Place fusible side of shapes against wrong side of appropriate fabric. Fuse in place following manufacturer's directions.

5. Cut out shapes on lines. Peel off paper backing.

If paper is hard to peel, tear paper to start.

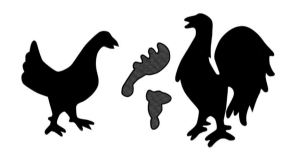

6. Position red combs under Chickens and Roosters.

7. Fuse in place on 6½" Background squares.

Fuse on 6½" squares for Large Barn Quilt

8. Blanket stitch around shapes by hand or machine. Stitch around black shapes with red thread and red shapes with black thread.

By hand:
Use two strands of embroidery floss.

By machine:
Place open toe applique foot on sewing machine. Set machine with narrow blanket stitch at 2.5 stitch length and 2.0 stitch width. Use needle down. Go slow around feathers and feet, pivoting with needle down in Background.
For a quicker finish, zigzag raw edges with invisible thread.

Hand blanket stitch

Machine blanket stitch

Sewing Checkerboard Border to Top

1. Place Checkerboard with seams in the same direction as they will be sewn.

2. Pin and sew Checkerboard to sides of quilt top. Press seams toward First Border.

3. Sew Corners to ends of top and bottom Checkerboard. Press seams toward Corners.

Large Barn Quilt	Small Barn Quilt
Chickens & Roosters	Stars

4. Pin and sew Checkerboard to top and bottom. Press seams toward First Border.

On Eleanor's Farm

48" x 57"

Background	1¼ yds
	(6) 14" x 18" rectangles

Black	**2 yds**
Lattice and Nine-Patches	(19) 2" selvage to selvage strips
Chicken/Rooster Bodies	Remainder of fabric

Red	**1 yd**
Combs	(2) 2" strips
Lattice and Nine-Patches	(12) 2" selvage to selvage strips

Binding	**⅔ yd**
	(6) 3" strips
Backing	**3½ yds**
Batting	**58" x 70"**
Paper-backed Fusible Interfacing	**1¾ yds**
Rooster	(3) 10" strips
Hen	(3) 9" strips

Making Chicken Applique

1. Follow directions for Making Chicken and Rooster Applique beginning on page 194.

2. Trace six sets of large hens, and six sets of large roosters. Make half of each looking in opposite directions.

3. Fuse to 14" x 18" rectangles and stitch in place.

4. Measure length and width of Background rectangles. Square up if necessary.

5. If Background is smaller than 14" x 18", cut Lattice to your measurement.

Making Nine-Patches and Lattice

1. Cut two red and two black 2" salvage to salvage strips in half.

2. Stack strips.

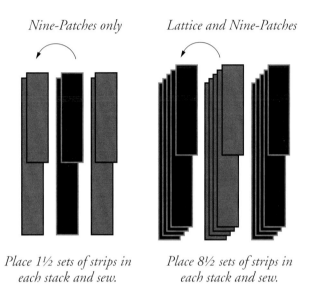

Nine-Patches only

Lattice and Nine-Patches

Place 1½ sets of strips in each stack and sew.

Place 8½ sets of strips in each stack and sew.

Half strips of both red and black are left over.

3. Assembly-line sew first two strips of each set.

4. Set seams with black on top. Open, and press seams toward black.

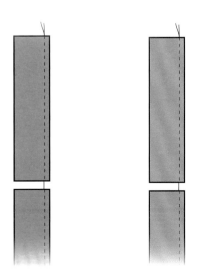

5. Sew remaining strips.

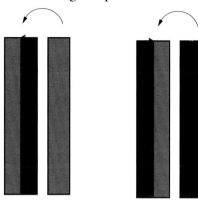

6. Press seams toward black.

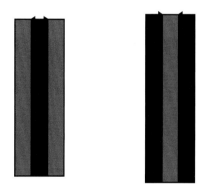

7. From Red/Black/Red sets, cut twenty-four 2" sections.

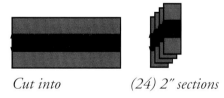

Cut into   *(24) 2" sections*

8. From Black/Red/Black sets, cut eight 18" sections, nine 14" sections, and twelve 2" sections.

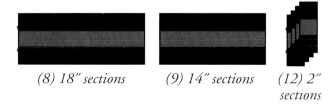

(8) 18" sections   *(9) 14" sections*   *(12) 2" sections*

Sewing Nine-Patches

1. Place twelve in each stack.

2. Assembly-line sew together into twelve Nine-Patches.

3. Press last seams toward center.

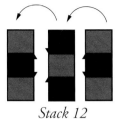

Stack 12   *Make 12*

Sewing Top Together

1. Lay out blocks two across and three down.

2. Place Nine-Patches and Lattice.

3. Flip second vertical row right side together to first vertical row. Assembly-line sew. Do not clip apart.

4. Assembly-line sew remaining vertical rows.

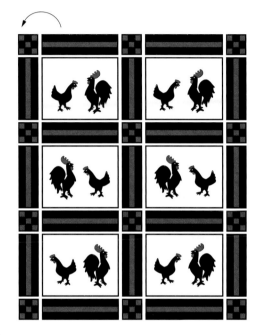

5. Press Lattice seams away from Background.

6. Press Nine-Patch seams toward Lattice.

7. Sew remaining rows, locking seams.

8. Machine quilt Lattice and Cornerstones. An appropriate stencil to quilt Background is a 2" x 3" chicken wire stencil from The Stencil Company, item SCL-023-12.

9. Bind.

10. Optional Eyes: Sew on buttons or make French knots.

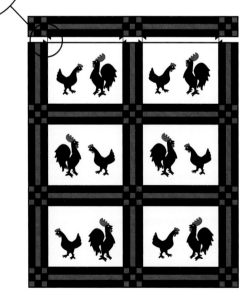

Finishing Your Quilt

Long Arm Quilting

Some quilters prefer to complete a top and send it to a long arm quilter. Follow these instructions if long arm quilting is your choice.

1. Clip loose threads. Make sure there are no loose or unsewn seams. Have top free of embellishments.

2. Press top and have it as wrinkle-free as possible. This applies to the backing fabric also.

3. The side measurements should be the same, and the top and bottom measurements should also be the same.

4. The backing fabric should be 4-6" longer and wider than the quilt top measurements. For example, if the quilt top is 90" x 108", then the backing should be 94" x 112" minimum.

5. The batting should be no less than 6" longer and wider than the pieced top measurements.

6. Do not pin the three layers together.

Some long arm quilters charge hourly prices depending on the density of the design, thread requests, and other factors. Others base the charge on the square inch size of the quilt. Your local quilt shop can often provide the names of local long arm quilters if you need help locating one.

Machine Quilting on a Conventional Sewing Machine

Layering Your Quilt

Follow these steps if you plan to quilt on a conventional sewing machine.

1. If necessary, piece Backing approximately 4"-6" larger than finished top.

2. Spread out Backing on a large table or floor area, right side down. Clamp fabric to edge of table with quilt clips, or tape Backing to the floor. Do not stretch Backing.

3. Layer Batting on Backing, also 4"-6" larger than finished top. Pat flat.

4. With right side up, center quilt on Batting and Backing. Smooth until all layers are flat. Clamp or tape outside edges.

Safety Pinning

1. Place pin covers on 1" safety pins with needle nose pliers.

2. Pin away from where you plan to quilt. Catch tip of pin in grooves on pinning tool, and close pins.

3. Safety pin through all layers three to five inches apart.

4. Use pinning tool to open pins when removing them. Store pins opened.

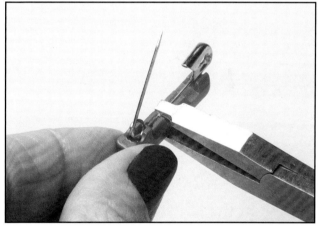

Quilt clamps

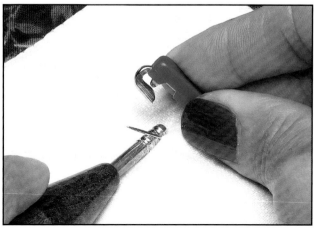

"Stitch in the Ditch" along Lattice and Borders

1. Thread machine with matching thread. Match bobbin thread to Backing.

2. Attach walking foot, and lengthen stitch to 8 to 10 stitches per inch or 3.5 on computerized machines.

3. Tightly roll quilt from one long side to Lattice. Place hands on quilt in triangular shape, and spread seams open. Stitch in the ditch along seam lines and anchor blocks and border.

4. Roll quilt in opposite direction, and stitch in the ditch along seam lines.

Walking Foot

"Stitch in the Ditch" around Blocks

1. With your walking foot, stitch in the ditch on seam lines around block.

2. If desired, quilt ¼" away from seams.

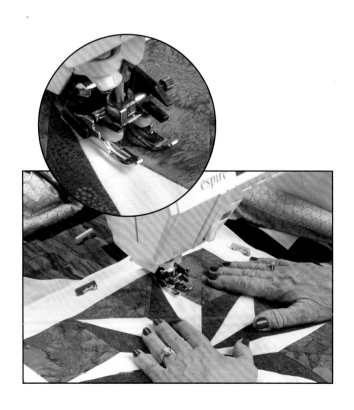

3. Mark checkerboard with hera marker and 6" x 24" ruler. Straight stitch on lines.

Quilting with Darning Foot

You can also stitch in the ditch with a darning foot so that you don't need to constantly pivot and turn a large heavy quilt as you do with a walking foot.

1. Attach darning foot to sewing machine. Drop feed dogs or cover feed dogs with a plate. No stitch length is required as you control the length by your sewing speed. Use a fine needle and regular thread in the top and regular thread to match the Backing in the bobbin. Use needle down position.

2. Place hands on edge of block. Bring bobbin thread up on seam or ¼" away.

3. Lock stitch and clip thread tails. Free motion stitch **on block**. Keep top of block at top. Sew sideways and back and forth without turning quilt.

Darning Foot

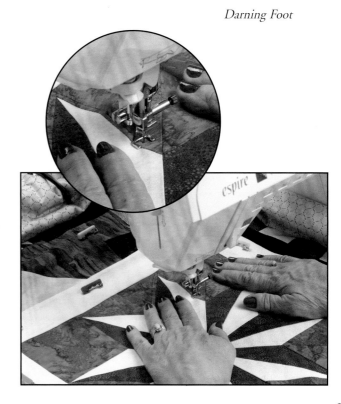

Binding

1. Square off selvage edges, and sew 3"
   Binding strips together lengthwise.

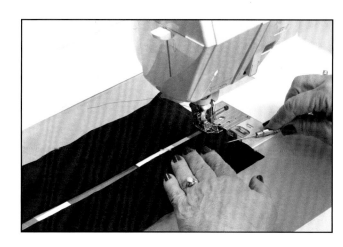

2. Fold and press in half with wrong
   sides together.

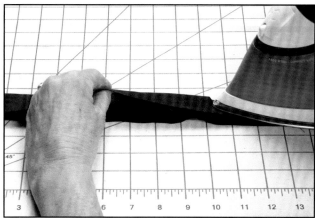

3. Place walking foot attachment on sewing machine and regular thread on top
   and in bobbin to match Binding.

4. Line up raw edges of folded Binding
   with raw edges of quilt in middle of one
   side. Begin stitching 4" from end
   of Binding. Sew with 10
   stitches per inch, or 3.0 to
   3.5. Sew approximately
   ⅜" from edge, or width
   of walking foot.

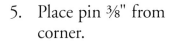

5. Place pin ⅜" from
   corner.

6. Stop stitching at pin, and stitch
   diagonally off edge of Binding.

7. Raise foot, and pull quilt
   forward slightly.

8. Turn quilt to next side.

9. Fold Binding strip straight up on diagonal. Fingerpress diagonal fold.

10. Fold Binding strip straight down with diagonal fold underneath. Line up top of fold with raw edge of Binding underneath.

11. Begin sewing from edge.

12. Continue stitching and mitering corners around outside of quilt.

13. Stop stitching 4" from where ends will overlap.

14. Line up two ends of Binding. Trim excess with ½" overlap.

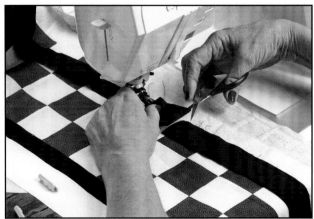

15. Open out ends and pin right sides together. Sew a ¼" seam. Press seam open.

16. Continue stitching Binding in place.

17. Trim Batting and Backing up to ⅛" from raw edges of Binding.

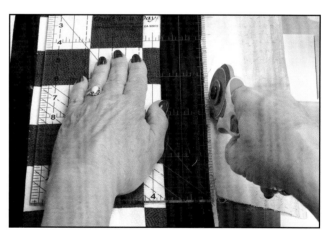

18. Fold back Binding.

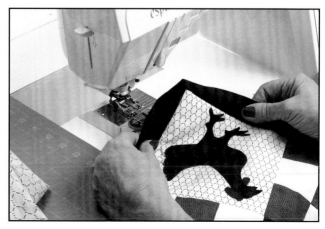

19. Pull Binding to back side of quilt. Pin in place so that folded edge on Binding covers stitching line. Tuck in excess fabric at each miter on diagonal.

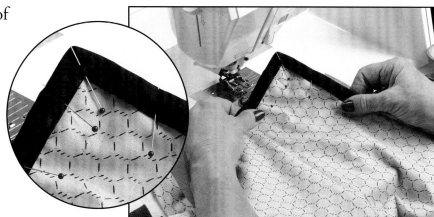

20. From right side, "stitch in the ditch" using matching thread on front side, and bobbin thread to match Binding on back side. Catch folded edge of Binding on the back side with stitching.

    Optional: Hand stitch Binding in place. Hand stitch miter.

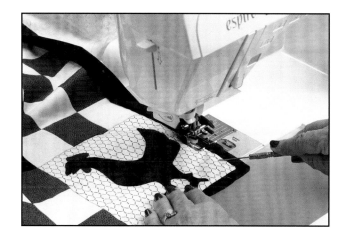

21. Sew identification label on Back.
    - place where quilt was made
    - year
    - name of quilt
    - any other pertinent information.

Tractor label made by Charleen Poppy

Student Quilt Gallery

O n the second Tuesday of every month in 2009, students gathered at Quilt in a Day in San Marcos,
CA to take a class from Eleanor Burns featuring barns and blocks painted on barns. Each month,
they learned how to make a new barn or block, and went home to make their own. Besides learning a variety of new techniques, they laughed a lot and became great friends! In December, students shared their finished quilts over lunch. As each quilt was shared, classmates were amazed at the creativity of each one. The
most impressed was Eleanor, because she enjoys their "spin" on what she taught them.

Flip through these pages and enjoy a few of the student's quilts, and you too will want to be creative
and personalize your own barn quilt.

Grandma's Wish for More Storage and a Bigger Space to Quilt

Elizabeth recently had to downsize to move into a smaller home. Her charming quilt expressed her desire for more space! Her blocks include Grandma's Fabric Barn, Grandma's Quilt Barn, Grandma's Flower Barn, and Applique Barn. But she was generous "building" a barn for Grandpa too! She enjoyed making the quilt, especially the fussy cutting, and adding her grandchildren to her Victorian House.

Elizabeth fondly remembers growing up with her grandmother and her big red barn in Indian Wells, CA. The barn is gone now, but Elizabeth has lasting memories.

Meadow and Sky

Linda fashioned her quilt to look like a window with black framing each of the blocks. The window appears to hang on background fabrics of green meadow and blue sky. Linda achieved a very interesting effect! She conveyed that she really enjoyed making the blocks, especially combining the little quilt blocks with the little barns.

Elizabeth Peay
Amie Potter
36" x 48"

Linda Holt
26" x 40"

Funky Chicken Quilt

This quilt was made by Lorna Proctor, who confessed to getting lazy and didn't want to make more blocks. She selected the most patriotic blocks, influenced by her friend Heidi and her own son, now in Young Marines. Not having the time to sew a checkerboard border, Lorna "cheated" with a checked fabric instead of a checkerboard. The finishing touch was the funky chickens she quilted all over, using a template with the same name!

Lorna Proctor
55" x 55"

A Good Team

Two close friends teamed up to make their quilts, even though they were miles apart!

Lorna Proctor and Heidi McFadden used to travel to Quilt in a Day together from Ramona, CA, a bit of a jaunt! Heidi moved to Colorado, and continued to keep up through Lorna. Besides being friends, Lorna was to long arm quilt Heidi's wallhanging!

Batik Barns

Heidi loves batiks, and finds it difficult to quilt with any other fabrics. Her two favorite blocks are the also the most challenging – the Harvest Star and North Star, done for her husband in Marine Corps colors of gold, red, and black. Heidi sewed a special barn like her mother-in-law's barn… and tediously paper pieced the star so it was authentic looking! Note that the center of the Broken Wheel block is a 3" Monitor Barn, sewn like the 6" one. Heidi loves the challenge! Good friend Lorna helped her out with some beautiful long arm quilting.

Heidi McFadden
Lorna Proctor
72" x 72"

The Hen Party

What an appropriate name for this quilt! Kathy focused on the chicken theme, using silk screened chickens, chicken wire fabric for lattice, and eggs on black for border fabric. She shared she used a piece of fabric she had forever – pulled it out, and everything came together! Even though she found some blocks challenging, Kathy said "it was fun to make". Her sister Dixie, who lives on a farm in Illinois, is the new recipient of this delightful quilt!

See setting for extra long quilt beginning on page 183.

Kathy Stolhand
Kathy Marsh
64" x 76"

Those Darn Barns

Sue Michalka's batik fabric makes her happy, with the colors matching the colors in her home. The quilt is so beautiful and nicely balanced, it will enhance any room. Sue thought the blocks would be challenging, but as she made them step by step, they came out well. The Y seams were the toughest, but she said it makes us better quilters for trying to push our skills. While she wouldn't have tried it on her own, Sue is proud of the finished results.

Sue Michalka
34" x 40"

When Pigs Fly

Julie Greenspan's whimsical quilt features a collection of pigs performing all kinds of antics. It's so entertaining to look at, it is currently hanging in the family laundry room! No one in the family likes to do laundry, so at least the quilt gives them a smile when they look at it. The mother of three teenagers, when they have an unreasonable request, Julie answers, "No, I don't think so. Maybe when pigs fly."

Friends and strangers donated pig fabric to Julie, including one friend who gave her five cartons. Her motto is to use humor to get through the years. When Pigs Fly brings a smile to your face!

Julie Greenspan
35" x 24"

213

Index

Thanks to our down on the farm quilting gals!

Piecers

2009 Block Party Ladies
Sue Bouchard
Marsha Burns
Julie Greenspan
Linda Holt
Patricia Knoechel
Chris Levine
Heidi McFadden
Sue Michalka
Sally Murray
Elizabeth Peay
Sue Peters
Lorna Proctor
Kathy Stolhand
Anne Tracy
Teresa Varnes
2010 Teacher Training Graduates

Long Arm Quilters

Kathy Marsh
Amie Potter
Lorna Proctor
Carol Selepec

Barn Sites

www.americanquiltbarns.com

www.barnquilts.com

www.countrybarnquilttrail.com

www.greenfieldhistoricalsociety.org

www.vacationaqt.com (Appalachian)

Teresa Varnes
Carol Selepec
40" x 40"

Sue Bouchard
Amie Potter
44" x 36"

Both of Sue's parents grew up on 100 year old farms in Southeastern Iowa. She wanted to celebrate their heritage by dedicating this quilt to them. The pictures are of her parents, Robert Hatch and Miriam Watts, their siblings, grandparents and great grandparents. Also shown is the actual "Century" farm Robert Hatch grew up in. Both of her parent's farms are still owned by family members.

Harvest Star – *The Old Threshers reunion in Mt Pleasant, IA is an annual event commemorating old threshing machines, steam engines and tractors. Sue's family still attends this celebration every year.*

Corn and Beans – *Sue's maternal grandfather grew corn and beans for both the family and the drift of hogs residing on the farm. She has fond memories of shelling peas for supper.*

Americana Star - *Americana Star honors both grandparents who served in WWI, Sue's dad, and his brother who served in WWII.*

Farmer's Daughter – *Sue's great grandmothers, grandmothers, mother and aunts were all farmers' daughters. It's a tribute to all of them!*

Quatrefoil Block – *Quatrefoil represents the traditional style of barn architecture found on Robert's farm. This barn was built by his ancestors.*

Hens and Chicks – *Sue's chore as a young girl was to gather the eggs every morning when they visited the farm. Her grandmother would then prepare breakfast when the men returned from their morning chores.*

Teresa Varnes
Amie Potter
36" x 36"

Starburst

Teresa set this quilt in orbit with 12" Harvest Star blocks on point and 6" Harvest Star blocks in the corners. She surrounded them with a striking blue narrow folded border.

Amie machine quilted a loop and star meander with feathers in the border.

Larger Than Life

Marsha Burns
51" x 40"

Exaggerated is the best descriptive word for Marsha Burns' quilt! Marsha was Eleanor's student in the 2009 Block Party. Three overstated cows hang out the Monitor barn door while a speckled hen just about as big as the cows looks on. A rooster as large as the gothic barn crows from the hayloft. Marcia claims she never follows a pattern – she is happy doing the unpredictable. Not into miniatures, she had fun with her embroidery machine stitching out huge vegetables. From the looks of things, she did have a great time!